ELECTORAL BAIT AND SWITCH

How the Electoral College Hurts American Voters and What Can Be Done about It

Bill Petrocelli

Prometheus Books

Guilford, Connecticut

(PB) **Prometheus Books**

An imprint of The Rowman & Littlefield Publishing Group, Inc.
4501 Forbes Boulevard, Suite 200
Lanham, Maryland 20706
www.rowman.com

Distributed by NATIONAL BOOK NETWORK

British Library Cataloguing in Publication Information Available

Library of Congress Cataloging-in-Publication Data

Names: Petrocelli, Bill, 1949– author.
Title: Electoral bait and switch : how the Electoral College hurts American voters and what
    can be done about it / Bill Petrocelli.
Description: Lanham, MD : Prometheus, 2020. | Includes bibliographical references. |
    Summary: "Electoral Bait and Switch is prescriptive and accessible to the general
    reader. If it is not challenged and overturned, we are likely to face a continual series of
    electoral and constitutional crises as the current Elector system discriminates heavily
    against minority and poorer voters. The winner-take-all method of allocating Electoral
    votes also results in large pockets of 'useless votes' and a system in which where your
    vote counts for far more than how you vote. Most ominously, evidence is now clear that
    the Electoral-Vote system has opened the door for voter suppression and manipulation
    of elections by domestic and foreign conspirators."—Provided by publisher.
Identifiers: LCCN 2020009529 (print) | LCCN 2020009530 (ebook) | ISBN
    9781633886582 (paperback) | ISBN 9781633886599 (epub)
Subjects: LCSH: Electoral college—United States. | Voter registration—Corrupt prac-
    tices—United States. | Elections—Corrupt practices—United States. | Political partici-
    pation—Social aspects—United States. | Minorities—Political activity—United States.
Classification: LCC JK529 .P49 2020 (print) | LCC JK529 (ebook) | DDC 324.6/3—dc23
LC record available at https://lccn.loc.gov/2020009529
LC ebook record available at https://lccn.loc.gov/2020009530

♾ᵀᴹ The paper used in this publication meets the minimum requirements of American National Standard for Information Sciences Perma-
nence of Paper for Printed Library Materials, ANSI/NISO Z39.48-1992.

CONTENTS

AUTHOR'S NOTE

As this book was going to press, the U.S. Supreme Court issued a decision on July 6 in *Baca v. Colorado* and *Chiafalo v. Washington*, (591 U.S. ___). These two cases are discussed on p. 85. The Court basically decided that states have the right to control how Electors select the President, cutting off any semblance of independence that Electors might have had. This decision does nothing to help the rights of real voters, and the Court does not address the unequal voting rights that permeate our current system. These cases reinforce what we already know: the only function of the Electoral College in modern America is to distort the popular vote for President.

To keep abreast of further developments about the Electoral College, please go to my website at www.billpetrocelli.com.

FOREWORD

Senator Barbara Boxer

When I retired from Congress in 2017, after spending twenty-four years as a senator from California, one of my last acts was to introduce a resolution that I still feel very strongly about: putting an end to the Electoral College. Like other Americans, I've now been watching presidential elections go awry in recent years, putting someone with fewer popular votes into the White House instead of the candidate who received the most votes. It's clear to me that this type of result undermines our democracy and wreaks havoc on our country.

I've known Bill Petrocelli for many years, and I know he feels as strongly about this topic as I do. I'm very excited that he has written this book, outlining the problems with the Electoral College and what we can do about it. He's been looking at this issue though several elections. Although the Electoral system had not altered the outcome of a presidential election during the entire twentieth century, Bill sensed that things were about to change during the 1996 election. He wrote a guest editorial on election day in the *San Francisco Examiner*, warning that Bill Clinton could win the popular vote but that the Electoral College could alter that result and give the presidency to Bob Dole. It didn't happen that day, but it did happen four years later in 2000, when Al Gore won the popular vote but lost the presidency to George

W. Bush. And after the 2016 election—when Hillary Clinton won the popular vote by almost three million votes but still lost the presidency to Donald Trump—it became clear to many people that something had to be done. This book points the way toward the badly needed changes in our presidential election system that would prevent this from happening again.

Many people are aware that the current Elector system is being used in a way that gives an unfair advantage to voters in some states at the expense of others. But what is not well known is that the system wasn't set up that way. The process designed by Alexander Hamilton, James Madison, and the other framers of the Constitution was not intended to operate the way it now does. They would probably be as appalled as anyone else to see how the Electoral College has been used as a process to override the popular vote. Over time, the Electoral College has become more and more distorted and fundamentally unfair to large numbers of American citizens. The value of a presidential vote differs from state to state, with the result that the voters in no two states have the same voting power. Voters in some states hold an advantage of almost three to one over voters in other states. Moreover, because of the way that Electoral votes are distributed throughout the country, minority voters, low-income voters, and city residents are heavily discriminated against. The winner-take-all rules of the Electoral College give rise to the "red-state/blue-state" maps that divide the country in a very unfortunate manner every four years. Taken together, these aspects of the Electoral College mean that some voters in some states have no real influence in determining who wins the presidential election. Every four years, the power to decide the race comes down to a handful of voters in a few states, leaving the vast majority of voters out of the calculation entirely. But maybe the worst feature of the Electoral College is this: It has simplified the task of foreign operatives and others who want to interfere with our presidential vote. The 2016 election showed how easily foreign law breakers can concentrate their efforts in just a few states and then count on the antiquated rules of the Electoral system to do the rest of the work for them.

There are ways that this system can be changed, and this book points the way forward. Fundamental change must be made no matter who wins the next election. If our nation gets through the next election without a distortion caused by the Electoral College, then we should consider ourselves lucky but still redouble our efforts to change that system. One thing this book makes clear is that the distortions created by the Electoral College affect *every* election—not just the elections in which the Electoral vote alters the outcome. The potential impact of the Electoral College is often an unfortunate part of every decision that is made in the run-up to presidential elections. The process for selecting candidates, the emphasis given to particular issues, the scheduling of campaign appearances, the expectation of voter turnout—these and many other components of a presidential election are affected by the antiquated Electoral College hovering in the background.

There's work to be done to change the Electoral system. And the place to start is with this book.

INTRODUCTION

How Many Votes Does It Take?

Quick quiz: How many real votes does it take to get one Electoral vote? Most voters know that the Electoral College alters the voting-power from one place to another, but what's the formula? If you're in Kansas City, Missouri, your vote for choosing an Elector is worth only about 70% of the vote of someone across the river in Kansas City, Kansas. Votes in Salem, Massachusetts, are worth about 95% of votes in Salem, Oregon. New Yorkers can improve the value of their vote by 14% by moving to Connecticut. One of the biggest impacts is in the west. In 2016, it took 257,847 popular votes in California to close one Elector but only 85,283 votes in Wyoming to do the same thing—a disparity of nearly three to one. It's the same situation across the entire country. The ratio of real voters to Electoral voters differs radically from state to state, and the differences seem to follow no regular pattern. So, what *is* the magic formula for converting real votes to Electoral votes in any given election? Is it based on the number of registered voters in each state? Is it related to the size of the turnout? Does it depend on whether the number of votes in each state reaches some threshold?

Actually, it's a trick question. The correct answer is both simple and shocking: There is no correlation whatsoever. The number of Electors in the United States is a fixed number, and it's not affected by how many people turn out to vote. Montana gets three Electoral votes, Iowa gets six, and Georgia gets sixteen, and it makes no difference whether residents of those states vote on election day or stay home or play golf. The total number of Electoral votes in the United States is 538, and that number hasn't changed since 1960—more than sixty years ago. The allocation of Electors among states is derived from a U.S. Census that is now at least nine years old. Under our current, distorted system, the number of Electors stays the same regardless of population shifts, get-out-the-vote efforts, political campaigns, voting patterns, or anything else.

This is a maddening system—made all the worse by the fact that it bears no resemblance to the Electoral College that Alexander Hamilton, James Madison, and the other framers had in mind when they wrote the Constitution in 1787. The framers intended a system in which only a few senior statesmen would gather to choose a President. They had no idea that America would some-day move away from that idea. They couldn't have predicted that Americans in the future would try to expand on the ideals of popular, democratic voting and put together a massive, quadrennial election to choose a President. And if they had foreseen anything like a popular election, they'd probably be shocked right now to see how their original Elector system has been twisted and distorted in a way that thwarts the results of such an election.

The framers created a system that is now frozen in the past, bearing no resemblance to the system we use now. They entrusted the selection of the President to a small group of senior states-men—men that they denominated as "Electors"—with the idea that these Electors would use their own judgment in selecting a President. The Electors would be appointed mainly by state legis-lators, and once appointed they were expected to act on their own. According to Alexander Hamilton (writing in the *Federalist*

Papers, no. 68), the Electors would be independent agents, beholden to no one, and "acting under circumstances favorable to deliberation." Consensus building within the Electoral College was supposed to be the key to its success, and this would "afford a moral certainty, that the office of President will never fall to the lot of any man who is not in an eminent degree endowed with the requisite qualifications." It's a system that we might compare today to a modern executive search committee—a small group of political insiders evaluating the best choice for President. The general public was not invited into the process, so there was no popular vote for the original Electors to consider or to override.

The Electoral system doesn't work like that anymore. The current Elector College is a cruel parody of the original system, and it serves only to distort the popular vote process that we now use to choose a President. Whatever virtue there may have been in a small, elite group of independent Electors selecting the person to serve as President, that system has long since disappeared. We've gone from a situation in which less than 1.8% of the population in 1788 cast any sort of vote to a point where more than 135 million people voted in the 2016 election. And we've changed from a collegial system, in which George Washington could be selected unanimously by the original group of Electors, to a system where all American citizens supposedly have the right to be heard in an open democratic process. Although the original idea of an elite selection process by Electors has long since disappeared, the appointment of Electors—that antiquated mechanism—still exists. The Electors of modern-day America are, however, an empty shell of what Hamilton, Madison, and the others had in mind. Today's Electors usually meet once for an hour or so and simply sign the paperwork that is placed in front of them. They are not expected to deliberate, consult, or evaluate candidates, or to do much of anything.

Most provisions of the Constitution have stood the test of time, but the Electoral system has not. This system has now degenerated to the point where we have the worst of both worlds. We have neither the original system, in which the selection of a President is based on the decision of an informed group of political insiders, nor a modern voting system, in which the candidate with the most popular votes wins the election. The Elector system has become such a caricature of its former self that it would almost certainly be as dismaying to the framers of the Constitution as it is to modern Americans. The only function of today's Electoral College is to distort the results of the national popular vote.

Although the law in America for many decades has been "one person, one vote," it has been ignored in the most important election of all—the vote for President. We are still using an Electoral system that was designed for a different purpose in a different era and hoping that it somehow won't get in the way of our democracy. For the entire last century, we were lucky. The antiquated Elector system didn't change the outcome of a presidential election during that one-hundred-year period, but unfortunately our luck has now run out.

I first had an inkling of the harm that the Elector system might do in the 1996 election, when it appeared to me that Bill Clinton might get more votes than Bob Dole but still lose the Electoral College. On election day that year, I wrote a guest editorial that appeared in the *San Francisco Examiner*, warning that this kind of anomalous, anti-democratic result could easily happen when the votes were being counted that evening. It didn't happen in that election, but it did four years later. In the 2000 election, while everyone focused on the mess created by the voting system in Florida, not nearly enough attention was given to the fact that Al Gore outpolled George Bush by 543,895 votes nationwide. Despite Gore's popular-vote victory, Bush was nevertheless declared President. That was the first time in 112 years that a candidate had become President after receiving fewer votes than his opponent. But it wouldn't be the last. It happened again sixteen years later, when Hillary Clinton received 2,868,686 more votes than Donald Trump. What had once seemed an anomaly was now starting to look like a normal feature of the system.

And that's not all. There's a temptation to look at the Electoral College as something that only hurts when it bites. There's a belief that, if we can just get through an election without the Electoral system altering the outcome, then we'll be okay for another four years. Certainly, an election in which the Electoral College alters the result is the worst harm that it can do. But there are other, systemic harms caused by the Electoral College on a continual basis, even when it is not doing something dramatic, like altering the outcome of a presidential election. It's like a low-grade fever: It may only spike on certain occasions, but that doesn't mean that it isn't hurting your health the rest of the time.

The Electoral system not only distorts the value of votes from state to state, but it also does so in a way that that greatly undervalues the votes of minority voters because those voters tend to be concentrated in the same large states that are penalized by the Elector system. This impact is made worse by the fact that the Elector system tends to lock in racial discrimination patterns and turn a blind eye to the very states that attempt to suppress minority voting. The system even distorts primary elections by forcing voters to choose between a candidate they prefer and one they think *other* voters prefer in those states that wield more voting-power during the general election. And even if the system were acting benignly, there is no escaping the fact the "safe-state/swing-state" phenomenon tends to depress voting turnout in those states marginalized by the Electoral College map. This lower turnout not only undermines the presidential elections but also has a strong, negative impact on down-ballot elections.

And if those factors aren't dismaying enough, consider this: The attack on our election system by Russian agents and others in the 2016 election only worked as well as it did because of the distortions created by the Electoral system. Election thieves—whether foreign or domestic—only have to find a state where the system is vulnerable and then switch a few thousand votes to pick up an outsized number of Electoral votes. It's a hacker's dream. You target your efforts to a few key states and then let the winner-take-all rules of the Elector system do the rest of the work for you.

I

THROUGH THE EYES OF THE VOTERS

ELECTION NIGHT AND ITS AFTERMATH

Americans go to the polls every four years, believing they are voting for a President. In November 2016, more than 135 million American citizens voted, making it one of the largest elections ever held anywhere in the world. And the stakes couldn't have been higher. Virtually every one of those voters walking into a voting booth believed that he or she was doing so in order to choose the most powerful leader in the world, the next President of the United States.

The voting itself was the last step in an all-consuming political process that lasted more than two years, cost more than $5 billion, and dominated American life like nothing else. There were more than one hundred primary elections and caucuses throughout the country, in which more than twenty-two candidates from the two major parties fought for the support of voters. The media attention throughout those many months was hard to avoid. Speeches, interviews, promos, panel discussions, commentaries, news clips, and advertisements were everywhere. The words and photos of the candidates appeared throughout the national airwaves, and those appearances careened through multistate markets, showed up repackaged in social media, and were replayed time and time again.

The highlight of the campaign was the more than fifty-seven candidate debates during both the primary and general elections, almost all of them receiving extensive media coverage. Fundraising was relentless, with endless pleas by mail, internet, telephone—many of them in the candidates' voices, all of them asking for money. Voters received repeated messages from nationwide sources, sometimes using the candidates' own words, urging them to get out and vote, spurred on by the repeated admonition that "every vote counts."

Then, on a Tuesday in November, everything reached a finale. Millions of people headed out the door to cast a vote in what they thought would be an election to choose a President. By evening, the votes were being counted, and those same voters waited to see who would get the most votes to become the next resident of the Oval Office.

And then?

And then, the voters were reminded by political professionals that they weren't *really* voting for President at all. Instead, the experts explained, they were actually voting for Electors—a group of faceless, unknown political functionaries who would *really* do the voting for President a month or so later. The names of most Electors existed only on a piece of paper filed somewhere in the various state election offices. Those names had been sent in earlier by the political parties, but the names they submitted were almost totally meaningless. The Electors named on the lists remained subject to change in most cases by party officials both before and after the election itself. Almost no one in the general public had any idea who those people were and what principles or public policy positions they might stand for. This realization came as a shock to most people. It's safe to say that no more than a tiny handful of the 135,649,280 people who voted in the 2016 election had any idea that they were handing over power to a group of 538 unknown people to select the next President of the United States.

Most people react with astonishment when they learn about the arbitrary way in which these Electors are chosen and how they go about selecting a President. *Do these people really decide who will be President?* Well, they used to do it that way, the experts say, but now it's different. *So what do they do now?* Now, things have changed. The Electors simply do what the political parties tell them to do. *So they no longer have the power to decide who should be President?* They do and they don't, the experts explain. They theoretically have that power, but no one expects them to use it. *You mean they're just supposed to show up to sign the election papers?* That's basically it. *Then why are they there at all?*

If the average voter listens to that explanation and mistakes it for a shell game, it's easy to understand why. Any semblance of fairness to ordinary voters goes out the window when the vote for President is funneled through the arcane rules of the Electoral College. A vote cast by a citizen in one state may be worth as much as three times that of a citizen in another state, and there are large numbers of votes cast in many states that become irrelevant in determining how the Electors go through the motions of naming a President. Over the years, the Electoral College system has morphed into a process that has become harder and harder to rationalize, and it is now a far cry from anything the framers of the Constitution intended. It's not surprising that most people react in astonishment when they learn how it really works. And once they realize that the Elector system has the power to change the outcome of an election and hand the presidency to a candidate who received fewer votes than his opponent—as it did in the 2000 election and then again in 2016—that astonishment turns to despair.

Those who try to justify the current Electoral system invariably miss the point. Their favorite argument seems to be that this is what the framers of the Constitution intended. However, even a quick reading of the *Federalist Papers* and other documents from that period shows the fallacy of that claim. What Alexander Hamilton, James Madison, and the other framers had in mind was that a collegial group of political elders would choose a President based on their own determination of the merits of the candidates. It was not until about thirty years *after* the Constitution was adopted—in the period leading up to the Civil War—that state legislatures tinkered with the Elector system to come up with what we have now. The changes they made at that time were done without any constitutional authority at all. But over time, those pre–Civil War legislatures managed to alter the Electoral College in a way that would both eliminate the independent power of the Electors and freeze popular voting into the restricted and unequal patterns that we have today.

Another favorite argument of the apologists for the Electoral College is that it was intended to give a slight edge to rural voters over city voters, who, it is argued, might otherwise overwhelm them. There is no historical basis for that claim. Even if it were true, however, the current Electoral College system doesn't really operate that way. While the Electoral system clearly does favor some voters over others, it does so in ways that are both arbitrary and discriminatory. But even if a justification could be dreamed up to support a form of "favoritism" for rural voters, the Supreme Court has shut the door on that idea. The Court has said repeatedly that voting is a fundamental right and that every vote should be counted equally, no matter where the voter happens to live. The rule of "one person, one vote" has been the law of the land for more than fifty years, and the courts have applied that standard to every form of election in America. The only election that has yet to be brought into compliance with this constitutional rule is the most significant one of all: the vote for President of the United States.

It is important to step back from this process and look at it through the eyes of the voters. Americans spend their entire lives being told that we live in a democracy. In a democracy, elections and public policy are supposed to be determined by the will of the people as expressed through a majority vote. We learn this as children, and we are constantly reminded of it by civic leaders and others throughout our lives. Even before the Supreme Court declared that the rule of "one person, one vote" should apply to all elections, most of us knew instinctively that this was the way that our government was supposed to work. That's the essence of democracy—the majority rules. But now we must face the jarring fact that things don't always turn out that way in the most important election of all. To add to their dismay, voters now learn that their vote could have counted more if they had cast it in another state or under other circumstances that are antithetical to majority rule. If you are a forty-year-old voter, you have now seen the concept of majority rule shredded before your very eyes in two of the five presidential elections in which you have voted.

When voters walk into polling booths, they think they are voting for a candidate who is named on the ballot—a Clinton or a Trump or a Bush or a Gore. But then the political insiders tell them that they are really doing something else: They're told that they're really voting for people who have the power to change the outcome of the presidential election and the course of history. So after being drawn into the long election process and living through all the intense political campaigning, voters are supposed to accept the idea that the end game of the process is nothing like what they had in mind.

That stark description of the current system elicits groans from most people. Many might sense a similarity between this type of process and the schemes promoted by hucksters and hustlers. If any business had come up with a promotion plan or a marketing scheme like our current Electoral system, then consumer-protection agencies all over the country would be after them to put a stop to it. Elections should be held to no less of a standard. When the key elements of the election process are hidden and the results can be distorted, the long-term result is an undermining of public confidence in the entire process. Right now, average voters can be forgiven for thinking they are the victims of a massive bait and switch.

THE MYTHS THAT PROP UP THE ELECTORAL COLLEGE

The Electoral College retains its grip on the American political system because of the myths that sustain it. These misconceptions have stifled public awareness of the problems and dangers of the Electoral system, and they have marginalized any efforts to change it. There is the myth that the Electoral College works fine in most elections and only creates problems for our democratic system on the rare occasions when it is contrary to the popular vote. This is a misleading and dangerous idea that has almost never been analyzed in depth. Another myth is that the current Electoral system we have now is the one that was intended by the framers of the Constitution. This rationale is frequently repeated by rote without any consideration of the way in which the Electoral system—and the nation itself—have changed fundamentally since the Constitution was written. The third myth is preemptive defeatism: Most people are led to believe that the only way to change the system is to amend the Constitution and that it's nearly impossible to drum up enough public support to do that. Both parts of that myth are wrong.

It's easy to be sucked into the myth that the Electoral College is a benign system that only occasionally goes wrong. The Electoral system lulled Americans to sleep for over a century, from the presidential election of 1892 and through the election of 1996. In each of those elections, the Electoral vote coincided with the results of the popular vote. It seemed like an easy thing to ignore—a harmless artifact of a different era. Throughout the entire twentieth century—two world wars, a major Depression, and two bloodlettings in Korea and Vietnam—the Electoral College seemed to have no impact on the course of American democracy. Midway through that period, the Supreme Court seemingly cut the constitutional underpinnings out from under the Elector system with a series of rulings guaranteeing the right of "one person, one vote" in all elections, but the Elector system itself was never challenged on that point in court. Perhaps it was because the Electoral College seemed quiescent. Americans had come to believe that it was irrelevant—or at least harmless.

All that changed with the 2000 presidential election. Al Gore beat George W. Bush in that election by 543,895 votes, but the Electoral College awarded the presidency to Bush. History repeated itself four elections later, when Hillary Clinton polled 2,868,686 more votes than Donald Trump, but Trump ended up with the presidency. Between those two elections, history almost repeated itself in reverse. If John Kerry could have convinced about 2% of Ohio's voters to support him instead of George W. Bush, he would have won the Electoral College vote even though Bush had won the popular vote by about three million votes.

Now that the Electoral College has altered the outcome of a presidential election twice in the last five elections—and come close to doing it a third time—the benign view of that system has come under serious scrutiny. It's become harder and harder to believe that it is just a historical artifact that only goes haywire once in a while. According to a recent study, "Inversions in U.S. Presidential Elections," conducted by political economists Michael Geruso, Dean Spears, and Ishaana Talesara (2019) at the University of Texas, elections in which the Electoral system distorts the outcome are more statistically likely than we might think. They estimate that, when the difference in popular vote is within a percentage point (which would be about 1.3 million votes, based on 2016 voter turnout), the probability of the Electoral College altering the outcome is about 40%. If the voting spread is about 2%, then the probability of an Electoral distortion is about 30%.

In fact, the Electoral College is not a benign institution under any circumstances. The Electoral College has had a major role in shaping our political institutions in a way that stifles full, democratic participation by a great many voters. The voting-power of citizens in presidential elections differs radically from state to state, and the states with the weakest voting-power are home to the most minority and low-income voters. The voting discrimination becomes even worse when you factor in that the "winner-

take-all" rules of the Electoral College that award a candidate all
of the Electors from a state, whether he wins it by one vote or one
million votes. This has created the phenomenon of swing states
and safe states, and the practical result has been to render many
millions of votes useless. Not surprisingly, these factors have combined to depress voter turnout in many safe states and to inflate
the importance of votes in a few swing states. The *Cook Political
Report* looked at the percentage of voters who participated in the
2012 presidential elections and found that voter turnout in the
swing states was 11% higher than the turnout for the nation as a
whole.

There are other structural problems beyond that. The system
distorts the presidential vote even further by basing the number of
Electoral votes for each state on the prior Census, thereby discou-
raging and hindering any efforts at voting reform. Behind the
scene, the Elector system is one of the biggest obstacles to extending the vote to previously disenfranchised voters. But perhaps
most pernicious of all is that the Electoral College provides a back
door through which hackers and international cyber-criminals can
attack and manipulate the system with minimum effort.

Another persistent myth is that the framers intended the Electoral
College to work this way, but that's simply not true. The original
Elector system was nothing like what we see today. The framers of
the Constitution created an indirect selection process, in which an
independent group of Electors was expected to meet and deliberate over their choice for President. In the words of Alexander
Hamilton, this "affords a moral certainty, that the office of President will never fall to the lot of any man who is not in an eminent
degree endowed with the requisite qualifications" (*Federalist
Papers*, no. 68).

Consensus building and deliberation: Those were the keys to
making the system work at the time the Constitution was written.
But none of that exists anymore. While it's true that modern-day
Electors still gather together a few weeks after the presidential
election, fill out some paperwork, and send it to the U.S. Senate,

almost everything else has changed. The method of nominating and selecting Electors has been radically changed. Their deliberative function has been curtailed, and their independence has been eliminated. The Electors were originally conceived as being a body of political veterans who could be expected to make a wise and responsible choice for President, but modern Electors are virtually anonymous, and they have been stripped of all real power. In most states, they can be removed and replaced even up to the day of voting if they show any signs of political independence. Electors are now expected simply to rubber-stamp a decision that has been made elsewhere. The shell of the system is still there, but any signs of life under that shell have long since vanished.

This change in the role of Electors occurred over several decades in piecemeal fashion. This book explores how this erosion of the role of the Electors occurred, but two things are abundantly clear:

1. This change did *not* come about through any kind of national, deliberative process. There was no reconvening of the Constitutional Convention and no effort to go through the amendment process set out in Article V of the Constitution. There was no conscious effort by national leaders to reexamine the presidential selection process. Instead, the degradation of the Elector system came about by a series of actions taken in haphazard fashion by state legislatures starting in the pre–Civil War years.
2. What replaced the original Elector system was *not* a victory for democracy. Although the changes that have been made over the years have added an element of popular voting for President, the voting system that emerged is anything but fair. Both the allocation of those votes and the power of those votes are frozen in a pattern that is inherently unequal and discriminatory for most Americans.

This gutting of the Electoral College might have been a positive step if it had resulted in a fair, democratic system of voting, but that's not what happened. Instead, the process of popular voting is filtered through a system that was never designed for popular voting. What has evolved is a system in which virtually every vote for president throughout the country is counted differently, resulting in a zombie-like version of the Electoral College that has no function in our current system other than to distort the result.

The third myth is in some ways the hardest to deal with. This is the belief that it is almost impossible to change the system. For some, there's a sense of defeatism that kicks in the minute you mention the words *Electoral College*. There's no way to change it, people sigh, because it is almost impossible to amend the Constitution to remove it. But this defeatism is misplaced. In fact, the current Electoral system is so far removed from what the framers originally intended that it almost spits out all the arguments needed to defeat it and replace it with something more equitable. The current Electoral College deviates radically from the original intent of the framers of the Constitution, and it has reached a point where it has become a lazy parody of itself.

Even more importantly, this system departs radically from the requirements of the 14th and 15th Amendments to the Constitution. These amendments, along with the Supreme Court cases interpreting them, stand for the proposition that all voters have to be treated equally. The Electoral College is now an outlier within the American system—a process that no longer plays by any of the rules that we expect in our democracy or that would be expected in any other democracy around the world.

Before giving in to any sense of despair about changing the system, consider these questions:

1. Would anyone today seriously propose a system that resembles our current version of the Electoral College, and would any country even consider adopting it?
2. Is the United States so ossified in its politics that we are doomed to live forever under a system that the rest of the world considers a laughingstock?

Changing the current Electoral system won't be easy, but it can be done. There are several groups already at work trying to make it happen. The proponents of change are not all coming at the problem from the same direction. Given the unique problem that the Elector system presents, you would expect people to try out different ideas and explore different avenues of change. Several constitutional amendments have recently been introduced in both houses of Congress to eliminate the Electoral College, and they have gathered much more support than similar efforts in past years. Eliminating the Electoral College has become a major campaign issue in the current presidential election, with several candidates seeking nomination making it a central part of their campaigns. An important effort is now underway by the National Popular Vote Project to circumvent some of the worst effects of the Electoral College by means of an interstate compact. There are also major litigation efforts working their way through the federal courts. In one case, the proponents are challenging the constitutionality of the winner-take-all rule that states have adopted for Electors, and in the other, the litigants are seeking to lift the restrictions that states have imposed on how Electors can vote. Throughout the country, the issue of changing the Electoral College has gained an audience that it has never had until now, with several major newspapers lending editorial support to changing the system. But the key to any change is public pressure. An informed, determined electorate will eventually make all the difference.

Perhaps the best chance for success will come if all these approaches to change the system are pursued simultaneously and reform efforts are pushed from every direction. Success in one strategy will help all the others. Progress toward an interstate compact may stir others to pursue a constitutional amendment more actively, and the reverse of that process may also be true. The possibility of success in the various legal challenges may create just enough uncertainty in the Elector system to generate a consensus in Congress and elsewhere that the system needs to be changed.

The most likely way the situation will change is when all the legislative, legal, and political avenues are pointed in the same direction.

There are other potential players in this drama who have yet to be heard from, and their voices could be decisive. Attorneys-general from some of the states harmed the most by the Elector system should be encouraged to file civil rights actions on behalf of the voters in their states. Civil rights organizations should be pursuing a legal strategy—state by state, if need be—to challenge the more egregious forms of discrimination. Congress has legislative power under both the 14th and 15th Amendments to enforce the rights guaranteed by those amendments, and that includes the power to enact legislation that could help secure voting rights. The House of Representatives on its own could set up a select committee charged with the task of documenting the harm caused by the current Elector system and developing ways to fight for the right to an equal vote in presidential elections.

None of this will work without an informed citizenry who is mobilized and determined to push for change. That's the point of this book. Hopefully, it provides readers with the information to encourage and support their political leaders to work for the needed changes. The time to end the Electoral College is now.

REFERENCES

Federalist Papers. The full text can be found at the Library of Congress archives: https://guides.loc.gov/federalist-papers/full-text#TheFederalistPapers-77.
Geruso, Michael, Dean Spears, and Ishaana Talesara. 2019. "Inversions in US Presidential Elections: 1836–2016." NBER Working Paper, no. 26247, Cambridge, MA, September 2019. https://www.nber.org/papers/w26247.

2

ONE PERSON, ONE VOTE ... EXCEPT SOME VOTES COUNT MORE THAN OTHERS

AN EQUAL RIGHT TO VOTE? NOT WHEN ALL VOTERS ARE TREATED DIFFERENTLY

Since 1962, the Supreme Court has consistently held that everyone's vote must be counted equally in every election. The rule is "one person, one vote," and the Court has made clear that citizens have a fundamental right to vote that cannot be impaired, restricted, or diluted in value. But that rule has yet to be applied in the most important election of all—the vote for President. There is no moral, legal, or logical reason the principle of "one person, one vote" should not extend to presidential voting, but instead, we are saddled with a system of grotesque inequalities and artificial restrictions. But before looking at the nightmare created by the current system of presidential Electors, it's important to take a brief look at what we are missing.

The Supreme Court has ruled in several cases that the constitutional right to an equal vote extends to virtually every voting situation. In *Wesberry v. Sanders*, 376 U.S. 1 (1964), the Supreme Court applied that standard to congressional districts, throwing out a state-redistricting plan in which one district had triple the population of the other. In *Reynolds v. Sims*, 377 U.S. 533 (1964), the Supreme Court struck down a voting system for a state legislature in which the districts had unequal numbers of voters. In *Moore v. Ogilvie*, 394 U.S. 814 (1969), the Court held that a requirement for gathering excessive signatures to get on the ballot also violated the "one person, one vote" standard. And in *WMCA, Inc. v. Lomenzo*, 377 U.S. 633 (1964), the Court required the upper house—as well as the lower house—of a state legislature to be apportioned based on population. In *Gray v. Sanders*, 372 U.S. 368 (1963), the Court struck down a system that diluted the weight of certain votes based on where the voters resided. In *Reynolds v. Sims*, 377 U.S. 533, (1964), the Supreme Court phrased the rule this way:

> Weighting the votes of citizens differently, by any method or means, merely because of where they happen to reside, hardly seems justifiable. One must be ever aware that the Constitution forbids sophisticated as well as simple-minded modes of discrimination.

While the rule of "one person, one vote" attempts to guarantee fair elections, it is also at its heart an individual, constitutional right. According to the Supreme Court, the right to an equal vote is a fundamental right, and that puts it on par with the right of free speech or the right of due process. Typical of the Court's statements about voting rights is this one from Justice Thurgood Marshall in *Dunn v. Blumstein*, 405 U.S. 330 (1972):

> In decision after decision, this Court has made clear that a citizen has a constitutionally protected right to participate in elections on an equal basis with other citizens in the jurisdiction.

Even a cursory look at the current Elector system shows that it severely distorts the value of individual votes and violates the constitutional standards laid down by the Supreme Court. It performs this sad task in several ways by allocating Electoral votes in an unequal fashion, by diluting the value of many votes, by linking the number of Electoral votes to the size of the population rather than votes actually cast, and by creating a pathway for hackers and intruders to interfere with an election. Each part of the Electoral system would raise a constitutional red flag on its own, but together they create a nightmare scenario that opens the door to abuse. None of these practices would be allowed in any local, state, or federal election in America. And there's no reason to think that the practices should be tolerated in the most important election of all—the election of the President of the United States.

Despite the rule of "one person, one vote," everyone's vote is counted differently in presidential elections. No two states are alike. How does this happen? It's because of the way the number of Electors is allocated among the states. Each state gets a minimum of three Electors, regardless of how small its population might be. Because of this, the number of voters per Elector is drastically higher in a large state like California than it is in a small state like Wyoming. Recall from the introduction: In 2016, it took 257,847 popular votes in California to choose one Elector but only 85,283 votes in Wyoming to do the same thing—a difference of nearly three to one. Thus, in California, three voters must go to the ballot box on election day to express their choice for President in order to have the same impact as a single person in Wyoming. So when it gets down to a battle between a voter in Wyoming, with his one Elector, and a California resident like me with my one-third Elector, it's easy to see who will win.

This is not to pick on Wyoming. It's a national problem because the Electoral system in the United States makes a mockery of the "one person, one vote" standard everywhere. Anyone who lives in any other big state, like New York or Texas, has the same problem. Under the current version of the Electoral system, the voting-power of people in any one state is different from that of voters in every other state. Depending on where you happen to live, the power of your vote may be dramatically different from someone just across the state line. To determine anyone's voting-power, you can simply take the total number of people who voted in that state (using, in this example, the 2016 election) and divide it by the number of Electoral votes allotted to that state. This gives you the number of votes that it takes to elect one Elector, and a comparison of those numbers will give some astonishing results. A voter in one of the four largest states (i.e., California, Texas, Florida, and New York) has only about 51% of the voting-power of a voter in one of the four smallest states (i.e., Wyoming, Vermont, Alaska, and North Dakota). If you live in Salem, Massachusetts, you have about 5% less voting-power than someone voting in Salem, Oregon. If you live in Springfield, Illinois, your vote is worth only 87% of someone in Springfield, Kentucky. If you live in Kansas City, Missouri, your voting-power is only about 70% of someone across the river in Kansas City, Kansas.

The capriciousness of this is system becomes even clearer when looking at the largest metropolitan areas in the United States. The seven largest Metropolitan Statistical Areas (MSAs) in the United States had 65,805,557 residents as of the 2010 Census. Of these seven MSAs, five of them include areas that overlap two or more states. Thus, people who live in one of these metropolitan areas could alter their voting-power simply by buying a new house or renting an apartment in another part of the area. Chicagoans who move to Gary, Indiana, would find that their voting-power has gone up 11%, but if they move back to the city, it reverts back to what it was before. Likewise, people in Philadelphia can increase their presidential voting-power by 11% by moving across the state line to Trenton, New Jersey, and commuting to work. Better yet, if they decided to commute in the other direction from Wilmington, Delaware, they'd find that their presidential voting-power had increased by an astonishing 108%. If you live in New York City, you improve the value of your presidential vote by 12% if you move across the Long Island Sound to Connecticut, but you decrease the value of your vote by 4% if you move in the other direction across the Hudson River to New Jersey.

In each of these situations, we're talking about the same people—people who vote every four years in the same presidential election but who just move around the area a bit between elections. And in each case, the relative power of their votes has gone either up or down—perhaps more than once—for no reason that has any logical connection with the election of a President. These types of changes in individual voting-power are both continuous and widespread, and they are becoming more common as the nation's population becomes more mobile. They create inequalities in voting rights that are arbitrary, capricious, and not reconcilable with any public-policy objective.

Whatever sense the Electoral system might have made at one time, it makes less and less sense in the modern era. Defenders of the system often claim that it benefits rural voters over urban voters and that this provides justification for its existence. The Supreme Court has made clear in many decisions, however, that you can't favor one group of voters over another simply based on where they live. But even if such a voting preference was constitutionally allowable, the current system doesn't come anywhere close to achieving that goal. Rural voters and urban voters are thoroughly dispersed in both large states and small states. In fact, there are far more rural voters in California and Texas than there are in some of the smaller, primarily rural states. Nevertheless, the rural voters in Texas, California, and other larger states are discriminated against just as much as the city dwellers in those states, because their voting-power is also weakened. The only way you can make a connection between the Electoral College and rural voters is if you assume that cotton growers in Texas and almond growers in California have a complete commonality of interest with potato growers in Idaho, cattle ranchers in Wyoming, and soybean farmers in Iowa and that a system giving an advantage to the latter group of rural voters also benefits the former group. This is the kind of intellectual leap that makes no sense, either under the Constitution or in real life.

Sometimes the defenders of the Electoral system come up with a variation on that argument by claiming that the framers of the Constitution were really trying to protect voters in certain parts of the country. This argument, of course, ignores the fact that the framers of the Constitution were not contemplating a popular vote for President at all. But even if they were, the Electoral system doesn't create any kind of a consistent regional pattern. The states where voters have the highest voting-power (i.e., states that require the smallest number of voters to select one Elector) follow no regional pattern at all. They are scattered throughout the country. Residents of the smallest states—those who benefit the most from the inequality of the Electoral system—include those in Alaska, Delaware, Hawaii, Montana, Vermont, and Wyoming. Far from constituting a regional pattern, these states literally span the width of the United States.

Another variation on the "regionalism" argument is the idea that the framers were somehow trying to equalize the influence of small-state voters by giving them a slight edge in the Electoral College. This is a highly oversimplified argument to begin with, but the implications of it have grown worse as time has gone on. The population of the United States has grown enormously over the last two centuries and dispersed in ways that no one could have anticipated. Thus, any slight edge that might have been intended for smaller states when the Constitution was drafted has now become a steep cliff over which any justification for the Elector system comes tumbling down. At the time the Constitution was adopted, the largest state (Virginia) had a population that was about twelve times that of the smallest state (Delaware). But that gap has now become more than five times larger than it was originally. Today, the population of the largest state (California) is about sixty-six times larger than that of the smallest state (Wyoming). In other words, any tinkering to equalize the influence of voters in smaller states with that of voters in larger states is even more harmful and unfair than it ever was.

But if protecting regionalism or rural communities were somehow a legitimate goal, then the voting discrimination that exists under the Electoral system totally misses the mark. The system protects political real estate—not people. According to the most recent U.S. Census, the average person in the United States is expected to move 11.7 times in his or her lifetime, and a large percentage of those population shifts occur across state lines. Data compiled by the University of Minnesota Population Center shows that migration in and out of every state in the union is heavy, and this movement extends across all regions. For example, in 2012 only 59% of people living in Kansas were born there, and 43% of people who *were* born in Kansas had since moved away from that state. Likewise, only 47% of the people living in Maryland were born there, while 34% of the people who were born in Maryland had moved elsewhere. The same pattern is true on the West Coast, where only 46% of Oregonians were born there, while 33% of native-born Oregonians moved someplace else.

The large numbers of Americans who have gone from state to state during their lifetimes have one thing in common: The value of their votes in presidential elections has changed every time they moved. The 25% of the population of New Hampshire who originally hailed from Massachusetts found the value of their presidential votes increase by 22% when they arrived in the Granite State. But the 6% of New Hampshire natives who moved in the other direction to Massachusetts were not so fortunate because their voting-power decreased by 18%. The same is true in every case of internal migration between the states. The 9% of Oklahomans who moved to Texas found their voting-power decrease by 12%, while the 6% of Oklahomans who arrived from Texas found that the value of their votes went up by 14%.

What these numbers show is that the Electoral system provides no systemic or even rational pattern for protecting particular classes of voters. Even assuming that such special protections are allowable under the Constitution, the current system only protects the ghosts of the people who may have lived in those regions centuries ago. Modern Americans have moved on, many of them to several states over the course of a lifetime. This migration defeats any rational purpose the defenders might ascribe to the system.

While for many Americans the inequality in the Electoral system is seemingly capricious, for others it is something more sinister. For those who are not as free to move about the country during their lifetimes, the impact of voting-rights discrimination runs much deeper. The Elector system—whether by accident or design—works to weaken the vote of low-income people and ethnic minorities. The places with the least amount of voting-power are the places with the heaviest concentration of racial minorities and recently naturalized immigrants. A December 8, 2016, article in *Wired* by Emily Dreyfuss analyzes the problem (the title sums it up: "The Electoral College Is Great for Whiter States, Lousy for Cities"). According to Dreyfuss, urban centers and their suburbs are where the majority of non-white Americans live, and they are the places that are hit the hardest by voting-rights inequality. Thus, the disparity created by the Elector system "undervalues the votes of people of color. That imbalance will only increase as migration away from rural areas to cities continues" (Dreyfuss 2016).

There is a basic problem of voting discrimination that arises out of the structural linkage between the Electoral system and the Census (this is examined in a later section), but a big part of the problem arises simply because of the way minority voters are distributed around the country. Because of the way Electors are allocated, the largest states in the union have both the *highest* percentage of minority residents and the *lowest* voting-power per person. This creates a double whammy for minority voters and casts the issue in a new light. Viewed from this perspective, it's clear that the discrimination in voting-power created by the Elector system overlaps with the broader problem of racial discrimination in America.

Racial discrimination in voting patterns adds a new layer of constitutional analysis to the problem. The Supreme Court has generally viewed the issue of voting inequality within the framework of the 14th Amendment. That amendment, the Court has said, gives each citizen a fundamental voting right (i.e., "one person, one vote"). But when the voting discrimination is more heavily focused against racial minorities, then an additional constitutional standard comes into play. The 15th Amendment says that the "right of citizens of the United States to vote shall not be denied or abridged . . . on account of race, color, or previous condition of servitude." The 15th Amendment has been the source of most of the voting-rights legislation that Congress has adopted since the 1960s. When there is evidence that a governmental process has a "disparate impact" on the rights of a racial minority, the courts are more likely to find that unlawful discrimination exists.

The Elector system clearly has this type of disparate impact. According to the most recent Census, the percentage of minority residents in the four smallest states (Wyoming, Vermont, Alaska, and North Dakota) averages only 18.4% of the population. By comparison, the percentage of minority residents in the four largest states (California, Texas, Florida, and New York) is approximately 51.2% of the overall population (with California and Texas being minority-majority states). You can argue whether this disparity is the result of accident or design, and the truth is that it is probably a little bit of both. Minority voters—particularly recent immigrants—tend to congregate in larger cities in larger states because those places are often ports of entry and areas with the best opportunity of employment. It's also probably true that many people in that category feel more welcome in larger communities than in rural areas, where they are often a much smaller minority. But whatever the reason, this disparity exists.

The disparate impact on voting rights becomes even more acute if you factor in the issue of low-income. While the correlation between racial minorities and low-income voters is by no means exact, discrimination against minority voters becomes undeniably worse when low income is added to the equation. The average poverty rate among the four largest states is about 16.5%, while the average in the four smallest states is lower, at 11.3%. When this discrepancy is added to the mix of other discriminatory factors, it simply intensifies the racial discrimination in voting caused by the Elector system. Although discrimination based on ethnicity and discrimination based on low income are two independent factors, in many cases, they act cumulatively to make the loss of voting-power by large groups of American citizens more intense.

When you look at how voting-power is distorted by where voters happen to live, there is another group of American citizens for whom the discrimination is the most intense. If you are one of five million or so U.S. citizens who live in one of the U.S. territories, your voting-power in presidential elections drops to zero. Although people born in Puerto Rico, Guam, the U.S. Virgin Islands, and the Northern Mariana Islands are U.S. citizens, their home islands have no Electoral votes. Hence, they have no voting-power at all in presidential elections. If residents of any of those islands—most of them ethnic minorities—want to vote in a U.S. presidential election, they have to pull up roots from their home islands and move to one of the fifty states or the District of Columbia to establish residence. However, the vast majority of these U.S. citizens, who may either be unable to move or who chose to remain in their home in those islands, get no vote at all.

There are strong elements of colonialism still at work in this situation, and they produce arbitrary results even for those citizens who have moved to the mainland but may later want to move back to the place where they were born. If you are a D.C. resident or resident of one of the fifty states, you can maintain your right to vote in your home state in a federal election, even if you move to a foreign country under the Uniformed and Overseas Citizens Absentee Voting Act (42 U.S.C. §§ 1973ff–1973ff-6, 39 U.S.C. § 3406, 18 U.S.C. §§ 608–609; UOCAV). In that situation, the states are required to let you to continue to vote even if you reside abroad for an indefinite period. But there's a maddening exception. If a citizen residing in one of the states wants to move—or move back, as the case may be—to one of the U.S. island territories instead of a foreign country, he or she loses the protection under the UOCAV Act. The result is that U.S. citizens from the mainland who want to live in a foreign country get voting rights in presidential elections that are denied to those who choose to live in a U.S. island territory.

When ethnic, racial, income, colonial, and similar issues are factored into the equation, the underlying discrimination of the Electoral system takes on an even more serious tone. The citizens who are discriminated against are not just numbers on a chart—interchangeable statistics that can theoretically be shuffled to justify an outdated theory about how America should choose its President. The discrimination against minority voters is real, and it is massive. The voters in small states, who already enjoy enhanced voting-power as a result of the misallocation of Electoral votes, are much more likely to be white voters than a simple numerical comparison would suggest. This is a problem that can't be ignored.

✲ ✲ ✲

THE DISMAL WORLD OF RED STATES AND BLUE STATES

In Barack Obama's first appearance on the national stage at the 2004 Democratic convention, he caught the nation's attention with his criticism of the "pundits" who "like to slice and dice our country into red states and blue states." He struck an important note with that statement, bemoaning the harm done by artificially dividing the nation in such a fashion. Unfortunately, this division seems to have gotten worse over the years. And the fault lies not just with the pundits. Most of the blame for the red-state/blue-state chasm rests on the distortions created by the Electoral College.

The red-state/blue-state maps dominate TV screens during every presidential election. They've even spawned an uglier cousin that pops up on the screen alongside them: the safe-state/swing-state map. These maps show a balkanization of American public life that has now taken on a life of its own, creeping into the national discourse on many levels. People who focus on these maps are constantly dividing and categorizing Americans into two groups. But maps are just maps; they only derive their power from an underlying distortion of our voting process. The red-state/blue-state maps that have wormed their way into the minds of most Americans would simply not exist if we were not trying to funnel the popular vote for President through the tortured system of the Electoral College.

The inequality of the Elector system begins with the unfair way in which Electors are allocated to different states, but it doesn't end there. There's another insidious feature that has been super-imposed on the system that causes the value of votes to vary wildly from one state to another: This is the "winner-take-all" rule that has been added to the Electoral system by state legislatures. Individual states began making this momentous change in the Elector system in the period before the Civil War, and they did so without any national debate or constitutional authority at all. Under this state-altered system, all Electoral votes are awarded to the winner of the popular vote in that particular state. (Two states, Nebraska and Maine, choose their Electors by district. But in both cases the winner-take-all rule applies within each of the two districts, so the way the system works is essentially the same.)

The winner-take-all system has been superimposed on a process where the Electoral votes are already unfairly allocated between the states. But with the addition of the winner-take-all process, the unfairness is magnified to a point where it is almost grotesque. These two factors basically act in tandem. Voting-power is unfairly distributed to begin with because of the way Electors are allocated, but the winner-take-all rule makes the situation worse by ensuring that many popular votes won't matter at all in the final tally. Taken together, these two features of the Elector system create a situation where votes in some parts of the country become wildly more important than votes in other areas. This perversity has now become a central part of the system. Under the

Electoral system, it is much more important *where* you vote than *how* you vote—or even *if* you vote.

Under the winner-take-all rule, the margin of victory in any given state is irrelevant. If a candidate wins a state by one million votes, then he or she gets all of that state's Electoral votes. But the same would be true if he or she won the state by one thousand votes—or even one vote. And it's not only the vote *margin* that is irrelevant under this system. The vote *total* makes no difference, either. If Rhode Island were underwater from a hurricane on election day and 50% of the anticipated voters couldn't make it to the polls, it would make no difference in the number of Electoral votes attributed to that state. Rhode Island would still cast four votes in the Electoral College. And the same would be true if most residents of Idaho spent the day fleeing from forest fires. Whether they showed up or not, Idaho would still get its four Electoral votes. In a sense, the Electoral votes keep moving on this dogged path, no matter what happens to real voters.

If you look closely at the red-state/blue-state maps or the safe-state/swing-state maps, you can see who the real actors are in our presidential election system and which of us are merely observers. If you live and vote in a "safe red state," then you—as an individual voter—are almost irrelevant to the outcome. The same is true if you live in a "safe blue state." In both cases you're on the outside looking in, while the voters in "swing states" decide who will be President. According to the National Popular Vote Tracker, there were only thirteen swing states in 2016 election, and those are the ones in which almost all the campaigning occurred. The other thirty-seven states (which comprise about 67% of voters nationwide) were largely ignored.

Political pros—along with election hackers and foreign intruders—follow the almost unbending logic of the Electoral College's distortions. They ignore useless votes. Presidential campaigns are not really a process of trying to win more votes than your opponent but rather an effort to find and coddle a relatively small number of voters in crucial places. And while they're scratching for every possible vote in swing states, political pros are simultaneously just trying to reassure the millions of other voters in safe states that they are not wasting their time on Election Day. Democratic strategists in 2016 didn't bother pursuing more votes in either Texas or California. Texas was a waste of time, because the Democratic nominee was perceived as having no chance of winning there. And California was a waste of time for the opposite reason: The Democratic candidate was almost sure to win, and any votes added to the winning margin would just be useless. And while Democrats were doing that, Republicans were making the same political calculations in reverse. They realized that there was almost no chance of their candidate losing Texas or winning California, so they directed their efforts to the swing states, where there was something to be gained.

Because of the distortions created by the Electoral system, neither party campaigns in a safe state. Nothing short of a "wave" election—one in which one candidate or the other would sweep the vast majority of the states—would shift a safe red state into the blue column or vice versa. There hasn't really been a wave election in American presidential voting since 1988. But even if that thirty-year trend reverses itself, it probably wouldn't make any difference in political strategy. If a candidate were to prove strong enough to turn Texas blue or California red, then political pros know that, in such a hypothetical election, their candidate would almost certainly have already won enough of the swing states to carry the Electoral College. The election would have been won— or lost—long before that wave hits the shore. There is almost no scenario in which it makes sense for a candidate to spend significantly more time in a safe state—whether it is a state safe for him or one that is safe for his opponent. Candidates might go to those states in the early days of the campaign in search of money, but they know that any extra votes they find there won't make a difference. There are few immutable "laws" in politics, but one of the laws of our Elector system is that you always ignore useless voters.

It's hard to argue with the logic of that strategy—and even harder to defend the perverse system that allows it to succeed.

Under our Elector system, the power of your vote is inversely proportional to the number of your fellow supporters in your state. It is also inversely proportional to the number of political opponents living there. If there are too many of either group in your state—whether allies or opponents—the value of your vote goes down, and you have almost no impact on who actually wins the election. Because the candidates can take you for granted, they have no incentive to campaign in your state or tailor their message to meet your needs or concerns. The only decisive votes in presidential elections come from those who live in the political Goldilocks zone—states where there are not too many allies, not too many opponents, and the political porridge is just right.

Most Americans are civic-minded enough to believe that they should vote in elections. It's their duty, they believe, and they somehow think that it will always make a difference. The Elector system, however, works against this sense of civic virtue at almost every turn. If most voters really stop to analyze how important their votes might be, then the arbitrary nature of the current system might overwhelm any good intentions. The swings in voting-power from one state to another are so great they defy the imagination.

Let's say you were an Al Gore supporter living in Florida going into the 2000 election, and you were trying to decide how important it would be to vote. In retrospect, it appears that a swing of 538 votes in Florida would have swung the state from George Bush to Al Gore, and the Electoral votes from that state would have put Gore in the White House. Because there were 5,825,043 votes cast for those two candidates in Florida, the addition of one vote in a race where the margin is that small could have a significant statistical impact. The value of each vote in that situation would be clear to our hypothetical voter, and the importance of voting would need no explanation. But let's say that you were a Gore voter living in Texas that same year, and you decided to go through the same mathematical exercise. You would soon realize that it would have taken a swing of 1,365,893 votes in Texas to put that state into the Democratic column and give Al Gore the White House. Your chances of affecting the outcome of the election would thus be staggeringly small, and you might be forgiven for asking yourself whether it was worth voting at all. But let's look at a third scenario: You decide to move from Houston to Miami a few months before the election, and you re-register as a Florida voter. A quick comparison of the voting margins in those two states shows something startling: By moving to Florida, your chances of influencing the outcome of that presidential election would have been 2,543 times *greater* than if you had stayed in Texas to cast your vote.

American democracy is missing something vital when numbers fluctuate as wildly as this. And this kind of disparity in voting-power is beginning to take its toll on voter participation in the election process. In the 2016 election, roughly 5% more voters went to the polls in Florida than in Texas. This is even more startling when you consider that Texas has a population that is about 25% higher than Florida (and it has nine more Electoral votes—thirty-eight to Florida's twenty-nine). Predicting turnout in any election is always a bit uncertain, but it's hard to escape the conclusion that the disparity in voter participation in that situation was affected—either consciously or unconsciously—by a sense that the outcome of the voting in a safe state like Texas was preordained. Voters might not have nearly the sense of urgency to vote as they might have in a swing state like Florida.

This decline in voter enthusiasm in safe states is borne out by several studies. The *Cook Political Report* looked at the percentage of voters who voted in the 2012 presidential elections and found that voter turnout in the nine swing states was 67%, and that was almost 8% higher than the 59.4% turnout rate for the nation as a whole in that election. Heavily contested states like Colorado (71.1%), Florida (63.6%), Iowa (70.2%), New Hampshire (70.9%), Virginia (66.9%), and Wisconsin (72.5%) all showed high turnout figures. This suggests that voters in swing states had more of a sense that they were doing something important than voters in other states might have felt.

This can be dizzying for the typical American voter. They find themselves either loved or ignored—there is almost no in between. Everything depends on where you live. If you live in a safe state, then there is virtually nothing you can do as an individual voter to affect the outcome of a presidential election. Your knowledge of the issues, the intensity of your political beliefs, and the degree of your civic involvement are all irrelevant. You could post a house sign, engage your neighbors, attend a forum, and do all the things you might do in a local school-board election, but you are probably wasting your time. In a presidential election, you are basically an observer to an election that is being decided somewhere else.

But if you are in a swing state, the opposite is true. Like it or not, everything is dumped on your shoulders. You may be blasted with constant political advertising that tries to cajole you or pester you into voting. Or, paradoxically, you may be the unwitting target of those who are trying to suppress your vote. And since 2016, we now know that you may become the victim of groups that will target you with massive disinformation. By election day, you may be sick of the whole process. But one way or another, the fate of the election ends up in your hands.

I've been voting in California all my life, and it's been considered a safe state almost that entire time. You watch the ebb and flow of campaigns being waged in other parts of the country, and you try to think of something that won't make you feel useless. That's why in 2008 I found myself squeezed into a small room north of San Francisco on a Saturday afternoon before the election. People were packed into every corner, holding typewritten lists of names they'd been given, talking as earnestly as they could on a set of telephones to voters across the country in Ohio—people who were complete strangers. I was part of a boiler room, trying to drum up votes for Barack Obama. The election was going to be decided somewhere else, and we were trying to make a difference. The people in rural Ohio on the other end of the calls were polite enough—at least the ones who bothered to answer the phone.

They were generally noncommittal about how they planned to vote—or about anything else, for that matter. They didn't know me, and I didn't know them. And neither of us really knew what we thought we could achieve through such an awkward, transcontinental conversation.

There's a general rule that can be drawn from this: If your election system forces you to make cold calls to strangers across the country to solicit votes for your candidate instead of having face-to-face discussions with your neighbors, then there's something seriously wrong with the system.

※ ※ ※

THE RACIST UNDERBELLY OF THE ELECTOR SYSTEM

There's a devilish element written into the Electoral College system that has helped perpetuate racial discrimination in American voting. It's a part of the system that has not often been discussed, but its effect has at times been devastating. The problem comes from linking the Electoral vote to the Census. It would be misleading to blame the Census itself for this problem. By and large, government officials labor mightily every ten years to achieve an accurate count of the number of people living in the various parts of America, and they often do so in the face of political interference. An accurate Census is essential for the allocation of public resources, determination of government benefits, and a host of other purposes. If done fairly, it is also an essential tool for determining the proper allocation of seats in the House of Representatives.

But the use of the Census as a basis for allocating votes in the Electoral College is a very different story. This unfortunate link of the Electoral system to the Census has helped perpetuate one of the ugliest chapters in American history: the role of slavery in the early days of the republic. Sadly, the problem didn't end with the Civil War because this same link also paved the way for Jim Crow laws and the suppression of African American voting in the South for more than one hundred years after the war.

The story begins with Article II, Section 1, Clause 2, of the Constitution, which says that each state shall have a "Number of Electors, equal to the whole number of Senators and Representatives to which the State may be entitled in the Congress." Because the framers linked those two numbers together, you have to look to another part of the Constitution (Article I, Sections 2 and 3) to find out how many members of Congress—and thus Electors—are allocated to each state. This process for allocating Electors created two distinct problems. One of them is apparent from the face of the document: Awarding Electors to a state based on the combined number of senators and representatives creates an imbalance, giving smaller states more Electors than they might otherwise be entitled to on the basis of population.

But it's the other, more hidden problem that deserves our attention here. The language of the Constitution that deals with the allocation of members of Congress (and, thus, the allocation of Electors) is found in Article I, Section 2, Clause 3. It is worth reading the first sentence of that clause to get a sense of what went wrong:

> Representatives and direct taxes shall be apportioned among the several States which may be included within this Union, according to their respective numbers, which shall be determined by adding to the whole number of free persons, including those bound to service for a term of years, and excluding Indians not taxed, three-fifths of all other persons.

This is the infamous Three-Fifths Clause—the portion of the Constitution in which the framers decided that African slaves would be counted as only three-fifths of a person for the purpose of allocating seats in Congress.

Most modern editions of the Constitution are quick to insert a note at this point in the text, saying that the Three-Fifths Clause was later changed by the 14th Amendment and is, therefore, no longer in effect. That's true, but given the way that the Constitution and its amendments are structured, the original language of the text remains in the document, even though it is later superseded by an amendment. It's probably just as well that it stays there in this instance because it serves as a reminder that the framers of the Constitution were just as prone as anyone else to serious lapses in judgment. The language of this clause—along with the fugitive-slave provisions in Article IV, Section 2—represents one of the bleakest moments in U.S. history.

The Three-Fifths Clause resulted from a crucial compromise between slaveholding states and non-slave states at the time the Constitution was being drafted. The issue in dispute was how representation would be allotted in the new Congress. Delegates at the Constitutional Convention realized that the problem was crucial enough that it could threaten the chances of forming a new union. Both sides claimed they wanted representation in Congress to be based on population, but that term meant something very different to each group. The non-slave states wanted representation to be measured by the number of free citizens in the state. The slaveholding states, however, wanted the entire population of the state—including slaves—to be counted in determining how many seats they would have in the new House of Representatives. The non-slave states balked at the unfairness behind that idea. They felt, quite rightly, that the slave states wanted to count their slaves for the purpose of determining the size of their congressional delegation, but they had absolutely no intention of allowing those slaves the right to vote. The slaves would simply be used to run up the number of representatives allotted to those states, even though they themselves would have no power to choose them. In the end, the non-slave states agreed to a compromise in which slaves would count as three-fifths of a person for purposes of determining the size of a state's congressional delegation. It was an act of political expediency that looks worse and worse in retrospect.

Although the Three-Fifths Clause has been superseded by later amendments, the structural problem it represents still has a pernicious effect. One of the lingering effects of this clause is the way in which it affects the functioning of the Electoral College. The precedent set by that clause is this: The number of representatives—and thus Electors—allocated to a state is based on the total number of people living in that state, even if a substantial number of those people are prevented from voting. Political leaders in a state can broaden their power by counting their entire population, thus increasing the number of representatives and Electors that they are awarded. But they can then turn around and tighten their control over those representatives and Electors by narrowing the number of people who get to vote for them. It's an enticing proposition for a political boss. You increase your power by securing a larger number of representatives and Electors, but you maintain your control of that larger delegation by ensuring that those added people are in no position to challenge your power.

Before the Civil War, this process worked almost automatically for the southern states. Three-fifths of their nonvoting slave population was counted to increase the size of their representation in Congress and the Electoral College, and the white voting population was then able to take advantage of that situation and enhance their power within the federal government. This disparity between population and voting-power accounts in large part for the strong and outsized political power that the southern states exercised within the union prior to the Civil War. But the problem didn't end with the Civil War, and in some ways, it got worse.

Following the Civil War and the adoption of the 13th and 14th Amendments, the slaves were freed, and African Americans living in the South were thereafter counted as whole persons—not three-fifths of a person. This added to the size of the official population of the southern states, and it allowed those states to claim an increased representation in both Congress and the Electoral College. But this increase came at a time when African Americans were *still* not allowed to vote. After Reconstruction was dismantled, voting rights for African Americans were severely restricted by the Jim Crow legislation that many of the states enacted. Even though the 15th Amendment seemingly granted voting rights to former slaves living in the South, the voting rights that were promised in that amendment didn't begin to materialize until about one hundred or so years later with the passage of the first civil rights legislation in the 1960s. During that long period, the descendants of slaves in many southern states had hardly any more voting-power than the slaves from whom they were descended. Nevertheless, those states claimed even more representation in Congress and the Electoral College based on the full size—not just three-fifths—of the African American population still within their borders. They did so while keeping voting-power and political control within the same narrow, white power structure.

The Elector system still awards states a built-in "voter-suppression bonus." Those who are in political control of a state can restrict the vote of their opponents as much as they can get away with, and they pay no price for such action in the national political arena. Under normal rules, the number of voters who would show up at the polls would be expected to have an impact on that region's influence in national politics. But that's not true under the distortions created by the Electoral College. No matter how unfair the voting restrictions may be and how many people may be harmed by those restrictions, the Electoral vote of that state remains the same based on the number shown in the Census. Because of this, the dominant political group within the state loses no influence in selecting the President, no matter how oppressive its voting rules might be.

The 1924 presidential election provides a startling example of how this works. In that year, Minnesota and Alabama had almost the exact same population and the same number of Electoral votes (twelve). But in that election, Minnesota had almost five times as many actual voters as Alabama (822,593, compared to 166,593). The small number of voters in Alabama was in large part due to the suppression of African American voters, but that systemic racial discrimination did nothing to weaken Alabama's political power in the Electoral College. Both states cast twelve Electoral votes. That intense voter discrimination actually enhanced the power of those in control of Alabama by giving them a greater proportionate say in how those Electoral votes would be cast. The presence of African Americans in their state was used to expand the number of Electoral votes, but the control over those votes rested in the hands of a small group of mostly white people.

The situation today may not be as dire as in the Jim Crow days, but the modern version of the Electoral College nevertheless undermines efforts toward voter equality at every turn. Imagine the response of a political boss when urged to extend voting rights to more people in his state. His first question may be, "What happens if I don't?" Sadly, the answer is, "Nothing much." His state will still cast the same number of Electoral votes, and he and his pals won't be penalized in the slightest unless the federal government goes through the arduous process of challenging them in court to expand voting rights. His second question may be, "What happens if I do?" The answer is that he will gain nothing by expanding the franchise and might even weaken his control over the Electoral votes that he now controls. It's pretty clear which path he is likely to take.

The Electoral College in its current, distorted version is a form of institutional racism. It may not have been intended to function that way, but it has the same depressing impact as the more deliberate forms of discrimination. Although there are laws in modern-day America designed to fight discrimination in voting, the Electoral College is a stubborn, institutional barrier that hinders that fight at every turn. It presents the same type of systemic, built-in discrimination that courts have seized on in the past to strike down voting restrictions.

We only tend to notice the Electoral College when it alters the outcome of a presidential election, but it really has an effect across the board. When those in power realize that any effort at voting reform may jeopardize their control over their state's allotment of Electoral votes, they have every incentive either to do nothing or to try to restrict the franchise of their opponents. And even if they focus only on suppressing voting in presidential elections, that same effort almost invariably affects other federal, state, and local elections within the state. Probably the best way to look at the Electoral College is to see it as the mother of all gerrymanders—affecting everything within its reach. The presidency is the big Electoral prize, and those who are determined to control their state's allotment of Electoral votes are likely to skew every other decision in a way that will guarantee that.

❋ ❋ ❋

THE ELECTOR SYSTEM IS AN ELECTION HACKER'S DREAM

The Elector system makes all the weaknesses and vulnerabilities in our presidential election process worse. Every mistake, every attack, and every effort at voter suppression is magnified and increases the chances that the election results will be distorted. Small, localized problems that might be absorbed into the larger national vote without changing the overall election result can become magnified into game-changing events when they creep into the winner-take-all calculations of the Electoral vote process.

In 2016, the voter turnout in Wisconsin was 3% less than it had been in the prior presidential election. That fact itself is suspicious. In 2012, Wisconsin was a swing state, and it had a voter turnout that was considerably higher than the nationwide average. But in 2016, Wisconsin was still a swing state, and the election in that state was no less hotly contested. Nevertheless, the number of voters dropped. The total in the 2012 election was 3,068,434 votes, but by 2016, it had dropped to 2,976,150—a decrease of 92,284 votes. Not only did the turnout drop in absolute terms, but it also dropped in comparison to Wisconsin's neighbors. Hillary Clinton lost the popular vote in Wisconsin by only 22,748 votes, and the closeness of that vote underscores the importance of figuring out what happened. Barack Obama had carried that same state in the two prior elections, so political analysts hovered over the

2016 results, trying to figure out what went wrong for the Democrats.

Of course, in analyzing voting patterns, there are usually multiple explanations, and several of them could be right to one degree or another. The voter drop-off in 2016 may have been due to voter apathy, and the drop-off in Democratic support may simply be explained by voters who supported the other candidate. But something seemed wrong. In 2016, the voting percentage had increased nationwide, so when Wisconsin was discovered to be counter to this trend, with a large voter drop-off, suspicions were aroused that there may have been some nefarious effort to suppress or alter the vote. It appears that this was true, and the Electoral vote system may have been an unwitting accomplice.

Some reports have indicated that Wisconsin was a particular target of Russian election-interference efforts during the 2016 election. *USA Today* reported on January 24, 2017, that Russian hackers had apparently "compromised the website of the 8th Congressional District Democratic Party as well as the sites of seven county Democratic party organizations" (Srubas 2017). CBS News reported on March 30, 2017, that Russian hackers had apparently created false "social accounts" during the election and that the fake news they were pushing looked like it was coming from "real voters in states like Wisconsin and Michigan" (Olsen 2017). Matthew Olsen and Benjamin Haas (2017) report, "Clint Watts, a counterterrorism expert and former FBI agent, testified in a March 2017 hearing before the Senate Intelligence Committee, 'Today, you can create content, gain the audience, build the bots, pick out the election and even the voters that are valued the most in swing states and actually insert the right content in a deliberate period.'" Watts cited evidence in his testimony that this sort of thing had occurred in Wisconsin.

Russian hacking could have had a significant impact on voter participation in Wisconsin. But the drop-off in voting in that state could also have been the result of a more local suppression effort. In its May 9, 2017, issue, *Nation* cited a study from Priorities USA that suggested that the decrease in Wisconsin voting may have been the result of that state's aggressive enforcement of a strict new law on voter IDs. The study showed several examples of voters who had been turned away from voting booths, many of them on technicalities. It also claimed that the "lost voters" included significantly more African American voters than the Wisconsin electorate generally. It's quite likely that many of these were Clinton voters. Priorities USA concluded that this voter-suppression effort had a big impact. Without that new law, Wisconsin turnout would have probably increased—instead of decreased—as it had in other states in the 2016 election: "If turnout had instead increased by the national no-change average, we estimate that over 200,000 more voters would have voted in Wisconsin in 2016" (Berman 2017). In a state like Wisconsin with a winning margin of only 22,748, an increase of 200,000 voters could easily have changed the outcome of the election in that state.

How does the Electoral College system enter into this picture? It simply makes every effort at tampering with the vote significantly worse. The Trump victory margin in Wisconsin of 22,748 was clearly a plus for his campaign, but the loss of those votes represented only 0.3% of Clinton's nationwide margin of 2,868,692 in the popular voting—a small dent in Clinton's otherwise successful campaign effort nationwide. But the impact of those same 22,748 votes in Wisconsin was anything but paltry when the Electoral vote was brought into play. That slim margin of popular votes allowed Trump to claim Wisconsin's ten Electoral votes, and as a result, he gained a big advantage in the Electoral vote count. One way of looking at it is this: The same 22,748 vote margin that gave Trump only about 0.3% of Clinton's nationwide popular-vote margin also gave him about 27% of his winning margin in the national Electoral vote. In other words, a small difference in the popular-vote margin in Wisconsin was magnified way out of proportion in the Electoral-vote count. In fact, the Wisconsin margin had an impact that was about *eighty times* higher in the national *Electoral* vote than in the national *popular* vote.

The Wisconsin Electoral vote alone did not provide the difference in the 2016 presidential election, but that state combined with two other swing states—Michigan and Pennsylvania—did make the decisive difference in the Electoral vote total. Trump's popular vote margin in all three of those states combined was 77,744 (Wisconsin 22,748; Michigan 10,704; Pennsylvania 44,292), and that gave him 46 crucial Electoral votes. However, Trump's combined popular-vote margin from those three states represented only 2.7% of Clinton's popular-vote margin nationwide. Nevertheless, this relatively small margin in popular votes in three states provided the springboard for him to secure the winning national margin in Electoral votes. Nothing like this would have happened without the dead hand of the Elector system interfering with the popular vote. These numbers illustrate one of the more perverse aspects of the Electoral system: It has the capacity to take a relatively small setback in the popular vote in one part of the country (in this case 77,744 votes out of a nationwide margin of 2,868,692) and give it an enormous, outsized impact on the overall election results.

This isn't the first time something like this happened. In 2000, the vote count in Florida was a long ordeal that kept the country on edge for several weeks. Even now, it's hard to sort through the incompetence, political influence, and likely malfeasance that went into the Florida balloting. But when it was over, the official result showed George Bush with a victory over Al Gore of only 537 votes. That was all Bush needed, because the Electoral vote system carried him the rest of the way to victory. But those 537 votes represented only a very small fraction of Gore's winning national margin in the popular vote—only 0.1% of Gore's winning margin of 453,895 votes. Nevertheless, that tiny margin gave Bush 25 of the 270 Electoral votes he needed to win. In other words, 0.1% of the popular vote netted George Bush 9% of the Electoral vote—a jump in value of about ninety times over his actual vote margin in Florida.

With all the focus on Florida in the 2000 election, no one paid much attention to all the other ways in which the Elector system distorted the popular vote in that election. As the recount in Florida was going through its laborious process, Al Gore stood at 266 Electoral votes—just 4 votes shy of the 270 needed to claim the presidency. But there were six other states that Gore narrowly lost to Bush (Arizona, Missouri, Nevada, New Hampshire, Ohio, and Tennessee), and the Electoral votes from any *one* of those six states would have given Gore the four Electoral votes he needed. And it is here that the Electoral system showed some of its most glaring perversity: Bush's *combined* popular-vote margin in those six states was less than Gore's national victory margin of 453,895. In fact, you could slip the Florida margin into that total, as well, and Gore would still have a greater margin in popular votes than the margin in all seven of those states combined. It may really be an understatement to say that the Elector system deprived Gore of a victory in the 2000 election because it appears that he was actually deprived of that victory seven different times.

So where do you look to cause trouble if you are a hacker? Some states are easier marks than others. And if you are intent on voter suppression or fiddling with the ballot boxes, some states will give you a much bigger return than others. One thing is certain: If you have election interference on your mind, then the Electoral College system is your best friend. In a sober analysis of the problem, Matthew Olsen and Benjamin Haas looked at the issues of electronic and other interference in presidential elections and warned, "Now, it's time to also examine the Electoral College through a national security lens." And their conclusion is this: "Ending the Electoral College should be central to the discussion" (2017). The winner-take-all feature of the Elector system provides a ready-made road map for those who want to manipulate future presidential elections. The strategy is to find a swing state that you want to target—a place where you can get the biggest Electoral-vote bang for your buck—and then concentrate your energies there.

You don't just have to take my word for it. You can see it in the methods used by the Russians who hacked into the 2016 presidential election. According to the indictment filed by the U.S. special prosecutor on February 16, 2018, against the Internet Research Agency and fifteen other Russian defendants, the defendants "posed as U.S. persons and contacted U.S. political and social activists" and then "communicated with a real U.S. person affiliated with a Texas-based grassroots organization." They were advised to concentrate on "purple states" in pursuing their efforts. After getting this advice from their American consultants, that's apparently what they did. According to the indictment, "defendants and their co-conspirators commonly referred to targeting 'purple states' in directing their efforts."

The indictment shows that the Russian conspirators chose Florida as one of the places to push their disruptive efforts. Florida was the state that had decided the election in 2000, and it was still a swing state that had the capability of doing the same thing in 2016. A small margin in popular votes in that state could—as it did in 2000—yield a big harvest in Electoral votes. Trump ultimately won Florida by the narrow margin of 112,911 votes. But to make sure that happened, the conspirators began their efforts in Florida around July 2016. Among other things, they allegedly used false American identities to organize March for Trump events, organized pro-Trump flash mobs, sent deceptive Facebook ads aimed at 59,000 Florida residents, purchased ads in a Florida Goes Trump rally, and leveraged their efforts through real grassroots organizations. They had been advised by knowledgeable politicians to focus their efforts on a swing state, and that's exactly what they did.

In most elections in recent years, there have been a few key states where a successful effort at voter interference could have swung the entire national result. The election of 2016 was just that, and there will probably be more. As electronic methods of interference become more sophisticated, we can expect to see this kind of effort again with even more technical wrinkles. If some future election tracks as closely as the 2000 election, then history shows that electronic hackers might have at least seven points of entry where the election results could be drastically altered. The Elector system that we have inherited from the pre–Civil War days makes this far too easy. In the future, those who are intent on stealing an election won't have to go through the messy, expensive task of penetrating all the nation's voting systems. They won't have to make the effort to reach voters nationwide with their misinformation. They can use any of a few key states to manipulate the local process and secure a few thousand votes, and that bit of thievery might be enough to decide the outcome for the entire nation. Future thieves—whether foreign or domestic—simply have to locate a state where the system is vulnerable and then switch a few thousand votes to pick up an outsized number of Electoral votes. It's a hacker's dream. You target your efforts to a few key states, and then let the winner-take-all rules of the Elector system do the rest of the work for you.

REFERENCES

Berman, Ari. 2017. "Wisconsin's Voter-ID Law Suppressed 200,000 Votes in 2016 (Trump Won by 22,748)." *Nation*, May 9, 2017. https://www.thenation.com/article/archive/wisconsins-voter-id-law-suppressed-200000-votes-trump-won-by-23000/.

Dreyfuss, Emily. 2016. "The Electoral College Is Great for Whiter States, Lousy for Cities." *Wired*, December 8, 2016. https://www.wired.com/2016/12/electoral-college-great-whiter-states-lousy-cities/.

Olsen, Matthew, and Benjamin Haas. 2017. "The Electoral College Is a National Security Threat." *Politico*, September 20, 2017. https://www.politico.com/magazine/story/2017/09/20/electoral-college-threat-national-security-215626.

Srubas, Paul. 2017. "Russians Suspected of Hacking Wisconsin Dems." *USA Today*, January 24, 2017. https://www.usatoday.com/story/news/politics/2017/01/24/russians-suspected-hacking-wisconsin-dems/97023222/.

Watson, Kathryn. 2017. "Russian Bots Still Interfering in U.S. Politics after Election, Says Expert Witness." CBS News. March 30, 2017. https://www.cbsnews.com/news/russian-bots-still-interfering-in-u-s-politics-after-election-expert/.

3

THE ELECTORAL COLLEGE IS A CARICATURE OF ITS FORMER SELF

How did we get into this Electoral mess?

The simple answer is that we've applied a constitutional provision designed for one thing to something for which it isn't suited. The "we" in that sentence refers mainly to state legislatures during the pre–Civil War period. It was the state-level politicians of that period who took it upon themselves—without any constitutional sanction or approval—to modify the original Elector system into something that would be unrecognizable by the framers of the Constitution.

THE ORIGINAL IDEA

The original Electoral College was nothing like we see today. The framers envisioned that political leaders in the various states would appoint Electors, who would then meet and decide among themselves who should be President. In a few cases, the Electors themselves would be elected by a very limited form of popular voting. But in such cases, the Electors usually stood for elections in their own name and not in the name of any particular candidate.

The Electors were expected to act independently and form their own judgments about whom they should select for President. The *Federalist Papers*, no. 68, assert,

> A small number of persons, selected by their fellow-citizens from the general mass, will be most likely to possess the information and discernment requisite to such complicated investigations.

According to Alexander Hamilton, the Electors would be independent agents, beholden to no one, and they would be "acting under circumstances favorable to deliberation" (*Federalist Papers*, no. 68). They should meet and make their choice with "as little opportunity as possible to tumult and disorder." Once appointed, it was anticipated that they would act without outside interference. Hamilton assumed there would be consensus building within the Electoral College and that would be a key to its success. The Electors' likely personal knowledge of the candidates, Hamilton argued, "affords a moral certainty, that the office of President will never fall to the lot of any man who is not in an eminent degree endowed with the requisite qualifications."

The system that the framers created was a compromise. Although some of those at the original Constitutional Convention might have preferred a popular election for President, they settled on this system instead. (As noted earlier, the convention was hopelessly split between those who wanted slaves to be counted for the purpose of determining the size of their delegations and those from antislavery states who were adamantly opposed to the idea.) They finally agreed on the idea of an indirect election through a system of Electors. As the Supreme Court dourly noted in *Gray v. Sanders*, 372 U.S. 368, fn. 8 (1963), "The electoral college was designed by men who did not want the election of the President to be left to the people." Whether the framers rejected the idea of a popular vote willingly or not, they proceeded to advocate forcefully for the Electoral system once it was written, and they fought for it in the debates leading up to ratification:

[T]he immediate election should be made by men most capable of analyzing the qualities adapted to the station, and acting under circumstances favourable to deliberation, and to a judicious combination of all the reasons and inducements that were proper to govern their choice. A small number of persons, selected by their fellow citizens from the general mass, will be most likely to possess the information and discernment requisite to so complicated an investigation. (*Federalist Papers*, no. 68)

The framers' idea of an Elector system seems strange today, but it probably shouldn't be dismissed out of hand. In modern parlance, what they were arguing for was something like a peer-selection process for choosing a chief executive. Officials at one level of government would meet and select the highest official for the next level of government. The selection would be done in much the same way as a modern parliament might meet and select a prime minister. The members would likely confer and reach consensus, and that process would hopefully be able to smooth out the rough edges of a system in which the members weren't appointed strictly on the basis of population. Electoral systems like this have been made to work in other governments. The President of Italy, for example, is chosen by an Electoral process that is similar to our original system. In theory, a system like this could be developed that might work fairly in the modern era. Nevertheless, Americans of today have become used to a democratic vote for President—or at least something they *think* is a democratic vote. Hardly anyone would want to go back to the framers' original idea.

The Elector system worked reasonably well in the United States for a time. During the first nine presidential elections, most Electors were appointed by state legislatures and functioned in a way that the framers might have anticipated. George Washington was selected unanimously by the Electoral College in 1788—an example of Electoral consensus at work. During that election, Hamilton himself served as an Elector, lobbying Electors in other states to build support for Washington. The 12th Amendment was adopted in 1804 to correct a flaw in the process (i.e., the need for Electors to cast separate votes for President and Vice President), but even that challenge didn't really disrupt the basic process. By 1820—thirty-two years after the Constitution was adopted—the consensus building was still at work to some extent within the Electoral College when James Monroe was selected as President by a vote that was just one short of unanimous.

THE DEMISE OF THE SYSTEM

The original Elector system was pieced together in 1787 by the framers in Philadelphia following a heated debate that lasted for a few weeks during the Constitutional Convention. Whatever its faults, it was a coherent idea that spelled out the original role of the Electors in our constitutional system. By contrast, the elimination of the original Elector system began a few decades later and occurred over a long stretch of time. It was done with almost no national debate at all, as different parts of the original system were discarded, one by one. The dismantling of the original Electoral system was done in pieces, state by state, without following any apparent plan or overall design. When it was over, those changes put an end to any important function that the Electors might have been expected to perform and stripped them of any real power. In this long effort to weaken the role of the Electors, no attempt was made to reconcile the changes with the essential role that the framers had assigned to the Electors when the Constitution was drafted.

As long as they kept the mechanics of the Electoral voting process intact, the state legislators that performed this drastic surgery seemed to feel that they had no obligation to maintain the original purpose behind the system. There was no reconvening of the Constitutional Convention, no attempt at proposing constitutional amendments, no widespread debate over the need for change, and no national gathering of political leaders to discuss what they were doing. These changes happened piecemeal. Although the changes fundamentally altered the way that the Electoral system was supposed to operate, the politicians who made the changes managed to do so without touching the language of the Constitution itself. The most important of changes occurred in the period leading up to the Civil War, and they have been kept in place and modified only in modest fashion since then. The overall effect of these alterations has been to change the Electoral College from a functioning political body to something that exists in name only—a shell of its formal self that is kept in place only to permit the Electors to sign the necessary paperwork.

What prompted these changes? There's no simple answer. In a sense, the states just changed the way they selected Electors because they had the power to do so, and no one was in a position to stop them. There were no federal laws in the pre–Civil War period that might have enabled a federal court to prevent such actions, and there was probably no motivation within the federal government even to try to do so. In the period leading up to the Civil War, the states—mainly in the South but also to some extent in the North—seemed more and more intent on asserting their own prerogatives in ways that were independent of the power of the federal government. The consensus that held the union together was beginning to fracture, and the Electoral system was fracturing along with it. The spirit of collegiality that had prompted Madison, Hamilton, and the others to create an Elector system that might function as a nationally minded body had largely disappeared.

These changes coincided with the rise of political parties during this period. Political parties—or political *factions*, as the framers disparagingly thought of them—were an anathema to those who drafted the Constitution. The dominance of the political parties proved incompatible with the original idea of how a President should be selected. The notion of an Electoral College, which would somehow step back from day-to-day politics to make a measured choice of the right chief executive, gave way to the winner-take-all rule, in which the winning political party chose all of the Electors in each state. Even though the changes made during this period increased to some extent the role of popular voting in the presidential selection process, the effect was illusory. This was not in any sense a period of voting reform. A closer look at the period shows that there was no effort to increase popular voting in general but only an effort to shore up the influence of those already in power.

THE IMMEDIATE RESULT WAS UNEQUAL VOTING RIGHTS

When the state legislatures implemented changes that weakened the Electoral College system during the pre–Civil War period, the result might have been the creation of a fair and equitable popular-voting system. But that's not what happened. The Electors were marginalized, but what replaced them was anything but fair. The Electors ceased to function as an independent, collegial body in most states (the one holdout was South Carolina prior to the Civil War, which continued to use the old system). In most cases the process of selecting persons to serve as Electors was delegated to the political party that prevailed in that particular state, and there were no significant rules or restrictions about who would be eligible to serve as an Elector. The states themselves retained almost no control over the people who might be chosen for the job, and over time the political parties used their power to both discipline the Electors and determine how they would vote. They also gained the power to replace Electors even up to and including the day that the Electoral ballots were supposed to be formally cast. Winner-take-all rules were put in place to make sure that the Electors voted as a group and that the winning party would get all the Electoral votes from that state. Eventually, the names of the Electors themselves were removed from most ballots, and the persons actually holding the job would not be disclosed to the voting public. Because they had no real function to perform, the Electors simply sank into obscurity.

But this weakening of the Electors did not result in the creation of equal voting rights in any of the popular elections that followed. In some cases, the opposite was true. The voting systems that the state legislatures created during this pre–Civil War period were in many ways a system of democratic voting in name only. The process was both limited and tenuous. By eliminating the independence of the Electors, the states theoretically put more voting-power in the hands of voters—but that power only extended to *some* voters. State governments during that period had the power to choose which groups would be allowed to vote, and this meant that a great many people were excluded from the process. State government officials were able to pick and choose which potential voters might serve their interests and then limit the franchise to those groups. Because there were no constitutional or federal protections guaranteeing any general right to vote during that pre–Civil War period, the process became simply a question of who had the political power within a state to set the rules.

Arguably, the form of limited voting during that period was worse than no voting at all. Prior to the Civil War, voting rights for many—if not most—people were largely ignored. The number of voters in presidential elections during that period was considerably smaller as a percentage of the overall population than today. In 2016, the number of votes cast in the presidential election represented 44% of the overall population, while in the 1836 election, the number of voters was only 12% of the total population. In the 1840 presidential election—to put it in even a starker perspective—the total number of votes cast for President (2,411,808) was outnumbered by the estimated number of slaves in the country at that time (2,487,355).

A look at the pre–Civil War period shows that suffrage was expanded or restricted like any other form of political patronage. Women were excluded from the vote almost everywhere. Property restrictions existed in certain states, and that requirement prevented many from voting. It comes as no surprise, of course, that slaves were excluded entirely from the vote during that period. Whatever motivations were behind these actions, the state legislatures were able to keep the electorate small by eliminating large categories of people who might otherwise have been expected to vote.

Some of the actions during that period were simply shameful. When the Constitution was adopted, free blacks had the right to vote in several states, but this right was later taken away. Prior to 1838, free blacks had the right to vote in Pennsylvania, but in that year, their suffrage was abolished as part of a deal that would remove property restrictions for white male voters. Free blacks were also allowed to vote in North Carolina until 1835, but that right was revoked in response to the Nat Turner rebellion a few years earlier. The voting rights of long-term immigrants moved back and forth wildly, depending on the level of anti-immigrant hysteria. In the 1850s, Connecticut and Massachusetts adopted literacy tests, while Rhode Island required naturalized citizens to wait two years before voting.

Until 1807, women had the right to vote in New Jersey, but that right was abolished as part of a compromise over the voting rights of aliens and the nontaxpaying poor. The story of this disenfranchisement of women was the subject of a recent article in the *New York Times* by Jennifer Schuessler (2020) and an exhibition at the Museum of the American Revolution in Philadelphia. Even during the period when they had the vote, women were hamstrung in many ways. The property requirements ruled out most married women because they had been forced to give up control of their properties to their husbands under the doctrine of "coverture." In 1807, the law was changed so that it explicitly limited the vote to white men while also loosening the property requirement:

> It is one of the dark ironies of American history that the broadening of the franchise to virtually all white male citizens coincided with the disenfranchisement of African-Americans and women. (Schuessler 2020)

None of these states would pay any political price for this practice of voter favoritism in the process of choosing a President. There was no reduction in Electoral votes for these or any other acts of callousness. Voting-power in the Electoral College for each state stayed the same no matter how many voters they had purged from the rolls or how many had been refused access to the voting rolls in the first place.

The point is not to relitigate history, but at the same time, we should be careful not to canonize the system implemented by the states before the Civil War. In moving away from the Elector system set up by the framers of the Constitution, the pre–Civil War legislatures took some steps to expand the vote, but they also took several steps backward. They were acting in an environment when there was no national protection of voting rights under either the Constitution or federal law, so they simply established—or revoked—voting rights as they saw fit.

As they were creating a very limited and restricted form of popular voting, the pre–Civil War legislatures were also leaving us with a version of the Elector system that is radically different from what the framers of the Constitution intended. And the problem doesn't just end with the original requirements of the Constitution. There is an even bigger problem reconciling this pre–Civil War system with the constitutional amendments that have been enacted since the Civil War. Today it is clear that the haphazard system of voting rights that followed the original weakening of the Elector system is wildly inconsistent with the "one person, one vote" rule that the Supreme Court announced almost sixty years ago.

✿ ✿ ✿

ELECTORS LEFT IN LIMBO

While looking at the pernicious effects of the current version of the Electoral College, it's worth pausing to take a look at the ridiculous, almost pathetic state of the Electors themselves. The original vision of the framers was that the states would appoint political leaders as Electors, who would then act independently to select the best candidate for President. But the Electoral College has now become a parody of that original idea.

Does anyone really care about the Electors? At this point, we're not talking about the Electoral vote system but rather about the Electors themselves—the 538 individuals from the fifty states and the District of Columbia who supposedly cast the actual vote for President. The names of the proposed Electors were hard to find anywhere before the November 2016 election. Unless you wanted to chase them down in obscure corners on state government websites, you'd probably never know who they were. More surprisingly, perhaps, the names of the victorious Electors—the supposed winners in the November election—were not readily available even after that election, when, theoretically, they were charged with the task of electing the President in the following month. A few Electors showed up in news stories during that period, when some of them made noise about bucking the system and not voting as expected. However, the complete list of Electors seems never to have been published by any major news source. (If you're curious, the complete list can now be found on Wikipedia: https://en.wikipedia.org/wiki/List_of_2016_United_States_ presidential_electors).

In the end, almost all the Electors voted exactly the way they were expected to vote. That's no surprise because they were all handpicked by political party leaders to act as loyal party functionaries—basically, to serve as a rubber stamp for decisions that would be made elsewhere. They weren't expected to meet and deliberate about the election or evaluate the qualifications of the candidates, as the framers had anticipated. Most of them would probably admit that their selection was more of an honorific for party loyalty than anything else. As the system currently works, their job has been simply to vote for the presidential ticket of the winning political party in their respective states and send the paperwork to the U.S. Senate. The whole thing is well choreographed in advance.

Even if Electors wanted to assert their independence, they can't under the laws of most states. In Alaska, for example, Electors are required to vote for the candidates of the "party that selected them" (Alaska §§ 15.30.020). In Alabama, Electors must certify that they will "cast their ballot as an elector for the candidates for President and Vice President for whom they agreed to serve as an elector" (Code of Alabama § 17-14-31). If they try to vote independently in Utah, they are "considered to have resigned from the office of elector [and] the remaining electors shall appoint another person to fill the vacancy" (Utah Code Ann. §§ 20A-13-301).

The names of the Electors don't appear on the ballot in most states, but it probably wouldn't make much difference if they did. If Electors don't show up for the meeting where they're supposed to cast their ballots, they can usually be replaced immediately by the ones who do show up. In North Carolina, for example, the Electors at the meeting can replace any Electors who are missing with any other state residents, and "they shall be deemed qualified electors to vote for President" (North Carolina Gen. Stat. §§ 163-209). In Pennsylvania, if an Elector is missing from the meeting where the vote is to be cast, the "electors present shall proceed to choose viva voce a person of the same political party" (25 Pennsylvania Consol. Stat. Ann. Chap. 14, §§ 2878, 3192, 3193). Likewise, if there is any vacancy at the gathering of Electors in Washington, those at the meeting "shall immediately proceed to fill it by voice vote" (Washington Rev. Code §§ 29A.56.320).

It's hard for anyone in the general public to find the names of the Electors because no one seems to think it's important to know who they are. They have been reduced to just names on a page somewhere—interchangeable on short notice or no notice at all. If they don't show up, then they are often replaced on the spot by those who do make it to the meeting. Their personal competence, background, or viewpoints become almost irrelevant.

Even scandalous behavior by an Elector doesn't seem to make a difference. Following the November presidential voting in Montana in 2016, someone in the media pointed out that one of the men chosen as an Elector had made some extremely anti-gay comments—suggesting on one occasion that LGBTQ people should be killed. Nevertheless, the party refused to remove him from the slate of Electors that was scheduled to meet in December to cast the official vote for President. The local GOP chairman just brushed off the complaint. His reason? According to him, the whole Electoral vote process was just a "ceremonial function."

❅ ❅ ❅

THE ELECTOR SYSTEM HAS FROZEN IN PLACE A SYSTEM OF UNEQUAL VOTING

Ceremonial or not, the long-term impact of the Electoral changes made by the pre–Civil War legislatures has been to freeze into place unequal voting-power throughout the country. This is what we see today in every presidential election. Even after some of the more egregious violations of equal voting rights in the pre–Civil War period had eventually been corrected, this problem has continued. The basic inequality in the allocation of Electors between the states has buried itself into the election system, and this is the system—with all its extraconstitutional alterations—that has been used by the states ever since. This process has never been subject to careful constitutional scrutiny, and we've slipped into it unthinkingly every four years without asking ourselves why. But this process has now proven itself to be the enemy of democratic voting, and the time for our unblinking acceptance is over.

There are two main vantage points from which we can look at the Elector system: from the front or from the back. We can either focus on it looking forward from the beginnings of our national history, or we can take a hard look at the system looking back from where we stand today. They may seem like different approaches, but both viewpoints yield the same result. Either way you look at it, the current version of the Electoral system looks unconstitutional.

If you look forward at this system from the vantage point to the framers, you see an Electoral system that functions in a way that the framers never intended. Article II, Section 1, of the Constitution says, "Each state shall appoint, in such manner as the Legislature may direct, a number of Electors." In keeping with that language, the state legislatures appointed the big majority of the Electors when the Constitution was adopted. But states don't do that anymore. The states have now delegated power to select the Electors to the various political parties, without any restrictions or standards about their background, capabilities, viewpoints, conflicts of interest, or anything else that might be pertinent to that job. On top of that, the states have given the political parties the power to remove or replace an Elector at any time—even after the popular election is over and, sometimes, even on the same day that the Electors are supposed to vote. It would stretch the English language to the breaking point to say that this is a situation in which the "state" is actually "appointing" the Elector.

There's a temptation to reach back in time and offer Alexander Hamilton and the other framers a good constitutional attorney who could take their case into federal court. Hamilton, as an Elector, actively lobbied Electors in other states to support his candidate, but under the current system there would be no room for an Elector like him to enter into any serious discussion or debate. Electors are forbidden by law—sometimes with criminal penalties attached—to change their votes. How long would Hamilton have been able to survive under this system? Our lawyer from the future would argue that these and other changes in the system were made without any attempt to amend the Constitution or to comply with the original legislative intent of the framers. One of the most hallowed doctrines of conservative legal jurisprudence is to seek out the legislative intent of those who enacted the rule, and on that score alone, the framers would seem to have all the arguments on their side.

The current version of the Electoral College looks just as unlawful when viewed through the other end of the constitutional lens. The state legislatures that stripped the Electors of their role as a deliberative body also froze into place a system of unequal popular voting. When they did so, they were operating in the years leading up to the Civil War, when there were no federal laws or constitutional protections of voting rights. It is an unequal system that is now frozen in time, and it reflects some of the worst practices that the Civil War was fought to change. The current Elector system has now become a mechanism whose only purpose is to deprive many citizens of the right to an equal vote in a popular election. This was never the intent of the framers. And since the adoption of the 14th and 15th Amendments following the Civil War, it has become more and more clear that this system of unequal voting in presidential elections is unconstitutional by almost any modern standard.

The constitutional infirmity begins with an unequal voting-power allocated to the citizens of different states—sometimes with discrepancies as high as three to one. By filtering the popular vote through a system that was not designed for popular voting, the current Elector system creates a major and continuing violation of the "one person, one vote" rule that affects almost everyone in the country. The constitutional issues become even more acute when you examine the way that the Elector system discriminates against minority voters. The voting-power of racial and ethnic minorities in presidential elections is far less than that of other voters, largely because where they reside in America. And by linking voting-power to the Census, the Elector system creates stubborn, institutional barriers to equal voting rights for minorities, raising the type of racial discrimination in voting that is forbidden under the 15th Amendment. On top of all this, there is the distortion caused by the winner-take-all rules of the Elector system. This was never contemplated by the framers of the Constitution, and it greatly intensifies the inequality and discrimination of all the other factors. As a result of this rule, votes in some parts of the country are greatly magnified, while other votes are virtually ignored.

How best to sum up this situation? The framers of the Constitution originally set up a system of Electors—senior statesmen appointed to choose the President. In the pre–Civil War period, the states, acting on their own, began moving away from that idea toward a system that involved some measure of popular voting for

President, but they never achieved a voting system that treated all voters equally or that was in compliance with modern constitutional standards. The result is an Electoral system that is stuck in a constitutional vacuum, lacking both purpose and fairness.

The current Elector system is like a rogue ship that set out years ago from its original anchorage in the Constitution. It is now floundering in the middle of the sea—unable to go back to its eighteenth-century moorings but equally unable to reach the safety of the constitutional amendments that have been enacted since then. It's a ship that's ready to sink.

REFERENCE

Schuessler, Jennifer. "On the Trail of America's First Women to Vote." *New York Times*, February 24, 2020. https://www.nytimes.com/2020/02/24/arts/first-women-voters-new-jersey.html.

4

PRESIDENTIAL POWER AND LEGITIMACY

When seen from the vantage point of equal voting rights, the current version of the Elector system is a disaster. But the view isn't much better through the institutional lens of the presidency itself. The President of the United States is the most powerful government official in the world, but much of that power comes from the deference and respect given to the presidency by others. Anything that calls into question the process by which the President is selected can weaken the office. "Whoever wins an election with the most support of the most citizens, should be the person who takes the office," Oregon senator Jeff Merkley told CNN on April 1, 2019. Anything else "diminishes the legitimacy of our president" (*Erin Burnett OutFront* 2019).

Legitimate accession to political power can occur differently in different countries. Political leaders can win office by simply winning more popular votes than their opponents. In France, the candidate who wins a majority of votes in a run-off election becomes President of the republic. There is no popular vote for President in Italy; instead, he or she is chosen indirectly by an institution designed just for that purpose, much like our original Electoral College. In almost every parliamentary democracy, the prime minister or other head of government is chosen by a majority of the national legislative body. In democratic institutions throughout the world, the head of government is chosen either directly by winning the popular vote or indirectly by the legislature or other body that is itself chosen by popular vote.

The United States is unique in having a system that seems almost designed to cast a cloud of illegitimacy on the election process itself. The United States spends billions of dollars to hold a quadrennial election that draws 135 million voters or more, and then it almost simultaneously invokes an arcane procedure that allows 538 virtually anonymous Electors to overrule the outcome of that election. It's that peculiar combination—the massive popular vote, followed by the potential overruling of that vote—that gives the system its maddening perversity. It's a classic form of bait and switch—the vote is held; the vote is taken away—and it is a process that is becoming more and more disturbing to Americans. And it's not just baffling to Americans. It leaves foreigners scratching their heads, trying to make sense of how our government really works.

The current version of the Elector system is an oddball process within American political life, and it has managed to sneak by for more than a century with rules that are different from any other election held in this country. For the last sixty years or so, the Supreme Court and other courts have looked at election procedures in a variety of situations at every level of government in our country, and they have ruled without exception that those procedures must comply with the standard of "one person, one vote." Voting is a fundamental right, the Court has repeatedly ruled, and it cannot be denied or impaired or ignored. But until now, no court has addressed head-on the issue of voting inequality in presidential elections. The irony, of course, is that this is by far the most important elected office in the country.

❋ ❋ ❋

THE MUDDLED DEFENDERS

The defenders of the current system come up with various arguments in defense of the Electoral College, but all their arguments run into the same problem. They are trying to rationalize a system that they know is a complete muddle. Almost none of them can say—without breaking into a smile—that the current Elector system is a well-thought-out political process that could be a model for other governments around the world to emulate. Instead, they rely on the trappings of constitutionality without much of the substance. Because no one can really argue that the current workings of the Elector system can be found anywhere in the annals of the Constitutional Convention, they try to find a rationale that they can retrofit into the Constitution. As they do so, they know full well that their best defense is simply to drag out the debate in the hope that it will go away.

One argument that defenders frequently make is that a presidential election was never intended to be a nationwide vote. Instead, they argue, the system was designed as a series of state-by-state popular elections that would then be filtered through the numerical arrangement of the Electoral College. There are many problems with that argument, but one of the biggest is this: The framers didn't intend that there be *any* popular election for President at all. In the system they created, they foresaw that most Electors would be appointed by state legislatures and would then come together and decide for themselves who should be President. Any attempt to claim that the framers wanted a popular election for President that would somehow be modified and number-crunched through an Elector system has no basis in history. That argument runs straight into the fact that popular voting for this purpose wasn't used on any widespread basis for many years after the Constitution was adopted.

At this point, defenders of the current system usually shift gears. They're likely to argue that the original intent of the framers was to have people vote on a state-by-state basis for Electors—not for the candidates themselves—and that the current system is perfectly compatible with that. But the flaw in that argument is just as glaring. The current system has degraded the role of Electors to the point where they are meaningless and almost anonymous. States have legislated away to others any real control over who can serve as an Elector, and they've circumscribed the power of the Electors to the point where they are not allowed to do much of anything—let alone, act independently to decide who should be President. In pointing to this rationale for the Electoral College, defenders refer to a process that hasn't existed in any serious way for almost two hundred years.

Another variation on that argument is the claim that state legislatures can dispense with the Electors and decide on their own how to cast the Electoral votes without bothering to go through a popular election process at all. That breathtaking claim deserves repeating: Some people claim that a state could suspend the popular voting for President within its jurisdiction and then simply declare who will be awarded the Electoral votes. You have to suspect that those who make this argument have looked at the sad charade of the current Electors and have privately concluded that the system doesn't really need Electors at all. From that, they've drawn the corollary that a state legislature can basically do anything it wants in allocating that state's Electoral votes. To call this preposterous is an understatement. The last time anyone tried to do this was about 150 years ago, when a few state governments were in the process of reconstituting themselves and coming back into the union after the Civil War. But in the modern era, with the enormous public interest in presidential elections, any politician who proposes suspending a presidential election for that sort of reason would probably find that his social-media accounts—and maybe his office, as well—had come crashing down.

And lest anyone feel that the current system can be preserved by suspending the popular election for President, that idea was basically slapped down, in of all places, by Justice Antonin Scalia in the case of *Bush v. Gore*, 531 U.S. 98 (2000). That case is remembered none too fondly today as the case that shut down the Florida recount in 2000 and, in effect, gave the election to George

Bush. However, in reaching that decision, the Court made clear that the days in which a state legislature can do anything it wants in a presidential election are over:

> History has now favored the voter, and in each of the several States the citizens themselves vote for Presidential electors. When the state legislature vests the right to vote for President in its people, the right to vote as the legislature has prescribed is fundamental; and one source of its fundamental nature lies in the equal weight accorded to each vote and the equal dignity owed to each voter. (*Bush v. Gore*)

Finally, the defenders of the current Elector system often fall back on the argument that an attack on the Electors is somehow an attack on the method of electing U.S. senators. But that argument is misplaced. Clearly, there is a great disparity in the size of the electorate for each senator, and the role and structure of the Senate is an important issue in any overall discussion of voting rights. But it's a subject that should be considered on its own merits and not confused with this one. Although the allocation of senators has a parallel in the allocation of Electors, the similarities end there. The Senate is a permanent, ongoing governmental institution in which members represent their constituencies on a multitude of issues. They are chosen in separate elections and then expected to deliberate, debate, and compromise with other senators in the creation of laws. Electors, on the other hand, have devolved to the point where they are merely an ad hoc group that meets for a few hours every four years to transmit the paperwork for a single presidential election. Each senator is an independent participant in the political process, free to vote his or her conscience on any number of issues and not under threat of instant removal by state or party officials. Electors, on the other hand, can be removed from their jobs by party officials in most states without much notice or fanfare. When you vote for a senator, you make a direct choice for the person to do that job on your behalf. When you vote for President—or at least *try* to vote for a President—you end up voting for an Elector you've never heard of. The only function of an Elector under the current process is to get in the way of the voting process for President.

The irony is that the analogy to the Senate might have made more sense at the time the Constitution was adopted because the framers viewed the Electors as independent political actors. But under the current version of the Elector system—where the role of the Electors has been reduced to rubber-stamping decisions made elsewhere—that argument falls apart completely.

Most defenders of the Electoral system don't really try to do so based on its merits. While there are those who like the extra voting-power that they may get from the way it is structured at the moment, there is almost no one willing to debate or defend the details in an impassioned, philosophical argument. You'll rarely see a defender of the Elector system get up in public and describe how it performs—as if the system were fresh out of the box—and tell an audience, "This is the kind of system our country needs!" Instead, the arguments are almost always defensive: "The framers intended . . ." or "The states were originally empowered to . . ." or "The country needed a system that . . ." For most defenders, their basic fallback position seems to be that this is the way the system has been operating, so let's try to find a way to be comfortable with it. They are probably smart enough to realize one thing: If they want to keep the current system, they're better off not talking about it too much. There's no way to extol the virtues of the current Electoral system and still pass the laugh test.

To taste the unintended hilarity that such a pro-Elector argument might evoke, take a look at Matt Ford's wonderful satire in the *New Republic* titled "The Case against the Popular Vote" (2019). He asks, "What would it sound like if someone proposed the Electoral College for the first time today?" Ford then provides a droll look at some of their likely arguments, such as "Under the popular vote, whoever receives the most votes will always win. The electoral college would finally end this tyranny of the majority by ensuring that candidates who come in second will occasionally become president."

* * *

THE ARC OF HISTORY

The Supreme Court has repeatedly ruled that an equal vote is a fundamental right under our Constitution. But are there degrees of fundamentality? If a voter has the right to an equal vote in a school board election or the choice of a town council representative, then wouldn't that same voting right be even more important—more fundamental—when selecting a President, who exerts much greater power over the lives of every person in the country? The Supreme Court has not suggested that there is any sliding scale to determine the importance of equal voting rights in various voting situations. But if such a test were ever attempted, it would become immediately clear that we as a society have been doing things backward. The vote for President is the one election for which we have not yet insisted on equal voting rights for every citizen, though the presidency has now become far and away the most important governmental institution that we have.

There are two important historical trends in America that have been gaining ground for some time, and they are headed on a collision course. The point of impact is the sad relic of the Electoral College. Presidential power has grown enormously since the Constitution was written, and it has now reached the point where it threatens to dwarf every other governmental institution. The power of the President is clearly far beyond anything that the framers of the Constitution could have contemplated. At the same time, there has also been a growing recognition of the importance of equal voting rights and how those rights need to be protected and expanded. Much of the impetus behind the voting-rights movement has been the crucial need to exert popular, democratic control as a corrective to the continuing increase in governmental power. These two trends are now at a crisis point. Either the right to an equal vote in presidential elections will be extended to all Americans, or the Elector system will continue to distort the system and hand the presidency to someone who may not have any sort of popular mandate. Whatever hesitation anyone may have about replacing the Elector system, they must be made to realize that, at this moment, the issue is more important than it ever was.

Every movement in our political history has been in the direction of increased presidential power. The framers could not have perceived the intimate, day-to-day impact that a modern President has with everyday Americans. The presidential powers enumerated in Article II of the Constitution are stark in their simplicity, and they hardly touch on the subjects that we now think of as central to presidential actions. The President is given the power, for example, to "make Treaties" and "appoint Ambassadors." But that simple enumeration of powers doesn't begin to describe the vast array of secret organizations, military installations, intelligence operations, and other activities that the President now administers throughout the world. Article II designates the President as "Commander in Chief" of the armed forces, but the framers lived in a world where the United States had no standing army, no weapons of mass destruction, and no foreseeable military threat that might affect the day-to-day lives of ordinary citizens. They could not imagine that modern Presidents—unlike their predecessors in the early days of the republic—would have the power of life and death over American citizens.

The increased power of the modern presidency in domestic life is no less significant. Modern-day Presidents affect the lives of virtually every person in the country through the administration of Social Security, Medicare, Medicaid, unemployment insurance, veterans' benefits, and a whole range of programs that millions of people depend on. Likewise, there are myriad agencies under the President's power, like the Internal Revenue Service, the Federal Bureau of Investigation, the Department of Homeland Security, and others that have the power to interfere with the daily lives—and even the freedom—of everyone in the country.

As the presidency intrudes more and more into everyday lives, the need for a fair and equal system of voting rights to choose the occupant of that office reaches the critical point. We've handed the President the practical ability to override the actions or circumvent the powers of virtually every other elected official in the country, so we have to ask ourselves this question: How valuable is our right of an equal vote in selecting other government officials when we are denied that same right in choosing the President?

While the powers of the presidency and the federal government have expanded in the last century, the voting rights of Americans—albeit far less dramatically—have been expanding, as well. Although rarely viewed as a competition, the expansion of voting rights in many ways has been an effort by those concerned with democratic governance to keep up with the growing power of the government. Voting rights have been expanded through constitutional amendments, legislative enactments, and judicial decisions. Although none of this effort has so far taken direct aim at the problems caused by the Electoral College, the thrust of these reforms is clear: Equal voting rights have been extended to more and more citizens in more and more voting situations. Each one of these constitutional and legislative enactments provides one more argument in support—another step forward—in the effort to extend equal voting rights to presidential elections. The effort to end the Electoral College is the last and perhaps the most important step in protecting our democracy.

The starting point for federal protection of voting rights is the 14th Amendment, adopted in 1868, and the 15th Amendment, adopted two years later. These two amendments expanded the right to vote and set the stage for the federal legislation to follow. Although they were adopted right after the Civil War, the implementation of these two amendments was delayed by the abrupt end of Reconstruction and the adoption of Jim Crow laws throughout the South. The full effect of these amendments only became clear with a series of Supreme Court cases and congressional enactments in the mid-twentieth century. Since then, federal regulation of elections—with respect to both voting rights and more mundane matters—has become a normal part of the system.

The 14th Amendment is the starting point for any look at equal voting rights. Section 1 says that no state shall "deny any person within its jurisdiction of the equal protection of its laws," and that language has been used by the Supreme Court as the foundation for its voting-rights decisions. The 15th Amendment was adopted two years later specifically to end racial discrimination in voting. That amendment says that the "vote shall not be denied or abridged" on the basis of race or color. The Supreme Court has cited the language of both amendments for voter protection in a variety of situations, and Congress has likewise used the power granted to it under these amendments as the basis for the authority to enact legislation protecting equal voting rights.

Although the 14th and 15th Amendments are the key changes that set the stage for the expansion of voting rights, they were not the only constitutional amendments that have moved the country toward equal voting rights. The 19th Amendment, adopted in 1919 and ratified a year later, says that the right to vote "shall not be denied or abridged on account of sex." The 19th Amendment more than doubled the number of eligible voters in the United States by extending equal voting rights to women. The 24th Amendment, adopted in 1964, prohibits any practice that prevents citizens from voting "by reason of failure to pay poll tax or other tax." By eliminating the poll tax, Congress and the states ratifying the 24th Amendment, implicitly recognized that discrimination against low-income voters was an unacceptable restriction on equal voting rights. Finally, in 1971, the 26th Amendment was adopted, further expanding the right to vote to anyone eighteen years old or older. These amendments all apply in all state and federal elections, including presidential elections. There is nothing in any of these enactments to suggest that these voting rights could be curtailed or weakened just because the election was filtered through an Elector system. They represent a growing awareness that fairness in voting is an important national priority.

Starting about sixty years ago, Congress also stepped into the role of protecting voting rights and promoting fairness in elections. The series of legislative actions by Congress over a period of decades represents a growing awareness that fairness in elections and equal voting rights is an important national concern—particularly as it concerns federal elections. The Voting Rights Act of 1965 (15 U.S.C. § 10101) is directed at candidates, campaign organizations, and others who have an active role in any election—including presidential elections. Likewise, the Federal Election Campaign Act of 1971 (52 U.S.C. § 30101 et seq.) governs disclosure of campaign finance and limitations on contributions to presidential and other campaigns. Presidential campaign contributions are also covered under the Bipartisan Campaign Reform Act of 2002 (116 Stat. 81–116). The National Voter Registration Act of 1993 (52 U.S.C. §§ 20501–20511), which extends the right of voter registration, also applies to presidential elections. The Uniformed and Overseas Citizens Absentee Voting Act (4 U.S.C. §§ 1973) provides voting procedures in presidential and other elections for citizens overseas and those in the military.

In every regulatory enactment in recent years, Congress has treated the election of the President the same way as it has treated any direct election. There's been no special carve-out—no special set of rules—that would exempt presidential elections from any of these requirements. Every step in the federal government has been to bring the voting process and presidential elections into line with other elections and to expand equal voting rights. The time to complete that task is now.

REFERENCES

Erin Burnett OutFront. 2019. Aired April 1, 2019, on CNN.

Ford, Matt. 2019. "The Case against the Electoral College." *New Republic*, September 20, 2019. https://newrepublic.com/article/155134/case-popular-vote.

5

HOW TO CHANGE THE SYSTEM

Eliminating the problem posed by the Electoral College is a unique and maddening challenge. It can be done, but those pushing for change must be flexible and imaginative in their strategic thinking to find the most effective way to do it. Instead of looking for a single, promising solution and then just pushing only for that, the proponents of change will most likely need to move in several directions at once to get where they want to go. What at times may look like a step sideways—or even backward—may be the right strategic move that will eventually lead to the desired outcome.

And defining the result is important. The goal is not just to rid ourselves of the Electoral College, although the demise of that bedraggled institution is probably inevitable. Nor is it just to get rid of those little groups of political insiders who gather for an hour or so every four years in state capitals to go through the ritual of signing the paperwork for the Electoral votes. The trappings of the Elector system will probably have to go eventually, unless the role of Electors is reduced to something that is strictly ceremonial and inconsequential. The real goal is more direct and more important: It is to establish a true democratic vote for the presidency. The pathway for getting to that point may wind in several directions, and the means for implementing a fair voting system are open to discussion, but there can be no argument about the ultimate objective. We must arrive at a point where every citizen gets an equal vote, and the candidate with the most votes becomes President.

Changing the Electoral system presents a constitutional challenge that is different than any we've ever faced. It may seem impossible at times, but at other times, it seems obvious and inevitable. The current system doesn't function in any way that resembles the original institution, and it hasn't done so for a long time. More than that, the current system is manifestly unfair to the great majority of the people in the country. Before anyone despairs of the difficulty of making the change, they need to step back a moment and consider that the current system is so wildly unfair that change eventually must happen. It's just a matter of time.

Securing free and equal voting rights is a civil rights issue on a par with every other civil rights battle that this nation has fought. None of these victories has ever come easily. Civil rights advocates endured several setbacks in the courts until the principle of racial equality was finally recognized by the Supreme Court in *Brown v. Board of Education*. The same was true in the fight for marriage equality and any number of other civil rights battles. The lesson of those struggles is that the advocates for change didn't get discouraged; they built their movement by going from one small victory to another, and they were clear in their goals. Nothing short of that kind of commitment will really succeed.

Those fighting for voter equality at this stage of our history have one advantage that other civil rights movements didn't have: The major, moral issue for voting equality has already been won. Unlike prior struggles, in which civil rights groups had to fight for recognition of their right to equality while fighting to implement it, this battle is waged under different circumstances. The principle of voter equality has already been established, and it has taken root in the public consciousness. The Supreme Court ruled more than fifty years ago that equal voting rights are fundamental under the Constitution, and that principle has now been accepted by almost everyone. While many, of course, just give lip service to the idea, there is almost no one who has the temerity to oppose it on principle.

So the fight to end the Elector system is a fight to implement an agreed-upon principle in the most important election process we have in our country. Once Americans focus on the reality that the election of a U.S. President is a single, nationwide exercise in democracy, then the philosophical and moral arguments against voter equality will be over. At that point, the old bait-and-switch techniques will no longer work. Voters will start to believe their own eyes every four years when they vote for a President, and they won't accept the arguments made by the apologists for the old system. Then the only real question will be tactical: How do we get from where we are at the moment to where equal voting rights can be implemented?

Even though Electors have now been stripped of all meaningful function, the details for counting Electoral votes still occupy about five hundred words in the 12th Amendment to the Constitution (which supersedes similar language in Article II). That presents a practical challenge, but it's not as insuperable as it might seem. The constitutional language mainly describes how the Electoral votes should be tabulated and sent to Congress, and those procedures are peripheral to the bigger issues. There is nothing in the constitutional language that talks about the purpose of the Elector system or explains or justifies how the current system has deviated so dramatically from the original system. The entire section deals with signing the documents, sending them to the President of the Senate, and counting the Electoral votes after they have arrived in Congress. All these steps were probably far more important at the time the Constitution was adopted, when the Electors were acting independently and it wasn't always clear in advance how they would be voting. Right now, however, it is little more than a procedure for handling the paperwork. But even though the process of casting and counting Electoral votes has long since become an empty ritual, the method of tabulation is still there in the Constitution. Anyone trying to bring fairness to the election of a President will have to deal with that fact and devise a way to repeal it or work around it.

There are different approaches to this problem, and groups trying to change the system have come at it from different directions. At first glance, some of these strategies seem diametrically opposed to each other. But the further you dig, the more you realize that they are all basically aimed at ending the current system and coming up with a more democratic vote. In some cases, that goal is more obvious than in others. On the one hand, those advocating a constitutional amendment are trying to address the issue head-on, proposing language that would repeal or substantially modify the Elector system. It's an approach that may be the easiest to grasp, but it is also the one that may be the most politically difficult to achieve because of the number of states that would have to ratify the amendment. On the other hand, those who are pushing the Interstate Voting Compact are approaching the problem from the opposite direction, using the Electoral College to lock in a commitment by Electors to vote for the winner of the national popular vote. That approach would require fewer states to approve it, but it would leave some questions unanswered.

There are other ways to work for change in the Elector system, and they involve a different set of tactics. Congress has the power under both the 14th and 15th Amendments to legislate enforcement measures that could bring about changes in the Electoral-vote process. How far Congress could go in changing the system depends on a number of factors, including the outcome of pending legal actions and other actions that might be filed in the near future. One active case challenges the authority of state governments to control the way Electors are allowed to vote. A federal court of appeals recently sided with these challengers, and if that decision is ultimately upheld by the Supreme Court, then it could upset the political calculations behind the Electoral system. Another group has filed federal court actions in four different jurisdictions challenging the winner-take-all rules by which states award Electoral votes. If those cases succeed, the Electoral system would be thrown into considerable disarray because each state would be forced to allocate Electors to each candidate in their state based on the percentage of the candidate's vote within that state. And still more litigation is possible, if not likely. The Electoral system could be attacked head-on in court by public-interest groups or by the attorneys-general from the states suffering the greatest voting discrimination. The argument in those cases would be that the 14th and 15th Amendments to the Constitution have rendered the current version of the Electoral system unconstitutional as a violation of the "one person, one vote" rule.

These solutions could all be viewed as competing strategies, but that is probably the wrong way to look at it. All these attempts at change are needed, and arguably we stand the greatest chance for success if we view them as complementary approaches that can build on each other and help strengthen the overall effort for change. Each has merit to one degree or another, but they all have their limitations. The Elector system is a rickety framework. If you move one piece, then the other pieces could start to fall. Success in any one of these strategies could help move the debate in a positive direction.

Each change—each added element of uncertainty—may force politicians to rethink the need for other changes. As more states ratify the Interstate Compact, politicians in states that are left out of the calculation could suddenly develop an affection for a constitutional amendment to straighten things out. If legislatures are forced by courts to allocate Electors among the various candidates, then Congress may feel the need to step in and enact legislation of its own. If federal courts begin ruling that Electors can vote any way they want and not be controlled by political parties, then party officials may see the virtue of abandoning the Elector system altogether. Each time the calculation changes for political insiders, opportunities open up for those pushing for change. Proponents must constantly rethink their strategy and shift their focus as new paths emerge. Hopefully they will pick up new allies along the way, but the goals will remain the same: achieving equal voting rights for everyone and making sure that the candidate with the most votes becomes President.

✿ ✿ ✿

CONSTITUTIONAL AMENDMENT

The most direct approach to changing the Elector system is through a constitutional amendment that would simply eliminate the system altogether and replace it with a popular-election process. This method is clear and straightforward, but it's one that's difficult to achieve at the moment because of the political challenges it would face. An amendment under Article V of the Constitution requires a two-thirds vote by each house of Congress and then ratification by three-fourths of the state legislatures. That means it would need the approval of a significant number of the smaller states in which citizens currently enjoy a greater voting-power in presidential elections than that of most other voters nationally. Asking a state to give up that outsized number of Electoral votes is a hard argument to sell.

Still, it shouldn't be ruled out. A constitutional amendment is worth pursuing if for no other reason than to keep the issue alive in small states. If you live in a small state and you agree with the thesis of this book, then it makes sense to confront your local legislators and discuss the issues—many of which they may not have considered. And as progress is made in other efforts to reform the system, the idea of a constitutional amendment may become more attractive even to people who are skeptical now. The amendment procedure is usually thought of as a very slow-moving process. The Equal Rights Amendment was adopted by Congress in 1972, and as of 2019, it still hadn't been ratified, but that's not always the case. The 26th Amendment, which gives equal voting rights to eighteen-year-olds, was adopted in 1971 and was ratified in less than four months. When the political will is there, the process can work quickly.

Although the Elector system has favored Republicans recently when it conflicted with the outcome of the popular vote, that situation could change. The Elector system put George Bush in the White House in 2000, but it almost evicted him in 2004. John Kerry came very close to winning the 2004 election through the Electoral College, even though he lost to George Bush by about three million votes nationally. In fact, it was just a few years ago that political pundits were talking about a Democratic "lock" on the Electoral vote. The Electoral system gives greater voting-power to residents of small states, and it is sometimes easy to conflate that fact with the idea that small states are "red states" that reliably vote for Republican candidates. But there are several small "blue states" (e.g., Delaware, Hawaii, Vermont) that have the same built-in advantage with respect to Electoral votes. Citizens in those states have far greater voting-power per person than citizens nationwide, so the political advantage doesn't always favor one party.

There are many concerns that residents of all states have in common: The growing vulnerability of the Elector system to foreign interference makes each state a potential target. In 2016, this assault came from the Russian government, but in future elections, a similar attack could come from the Russians as well as any number of foreign or domestic adversaries. It could be aimed at the voting system in any one state or several states. It's probably safe to assume that all voters in the United States—whether from large or small states—want to protect the country from that type of interference.

There are still other factors that may put many of us in the same unlikely boat. The perverse impact of the winner-take-all rule in the allocation of Electoral votes can affect voters on different sides of the political aisle. Residents of safe blue states and safe red states both find themselves ignored during a political campaign, and this can happen whether they live in a large or small state. When the polls close on election night and the vote count starts moving westward, the results of the Electoral College are usually announced before the votes are counted in the west.

That leaves many of us feeling useless, regardless of our political affiliation.

A constitutional amendment would do two things, and both of them are important. The first thing, of course, is to put an end to the current Electoral system. There are several ways an amendment could be worded, but the precise language is less important than the result. Whichever way it is worded, it would need to end the current system or modify it in such a way that it doesn't interfere with the popular vote or create a system of unequal voting rights. The experience with most constitutional amendments is that they are written as general pronouncements, with the expectation that the specifics will be carried out by Congress through appropriate legislation.

But there's a second function of a constitutional amendment that is equally important, and it may require more extended language within the amendment itself. It's not enough simply to abolish the Electoral College, because that antiquated system needs to be replaced by something else. Unlike the provisions found in many other amendments, this one is not likely to be self-executing. Some amendments (e.g., the 19th Amendment's prohibition against voting discrimination "on account of sex") focus almost entirely on prohibited governmental actions. A state could comply with the 19th Amendment by ending any procedures that exclude women. But when the Electoral College is changed or abolished, something will have to replace it. Any amendment making that change would have to contain at least the outline of the new procedure that the federal government should put in place to conduct a fair election. Some of the details could be spelled out in the amendment itself, but significant aspects of the system could also be left to Congress to work out through legislation.

Several constitutional amendments have recently been proposed to end the Elector system, and any final version of an amendment approved by Congress would inevitably go through several changes. One promising amendment was proposed by Senator Brian Schatz (Democrat, Hawaii) on April 2, 2019, with the support of Senators Dick Durbin (Democrat, Illinois), Dianne Feinstein (Democrat, California), and Kirsten Gillibrand (Democrat, New York). This amendment would create a new constitutional system for electing a President and provide a good look at how that new system might ultimately function. Under the Schatz proposal, the Electoral College would be repealed, and the voters themselves would become the "Electors":

Section 1. The President and Vice President shall be elected by the people of the several States and the district constituting the seat of government of the United States.

Section 2. The electors in each State shall have the qualifications requisite for electors of the most populous branch of the legislature of the State. . . .

Section 3. Each elector shall cast a single vote for two persons who have consented to the joining of their names as candidates for President and Vice President. . . .

Section 4. The pair of candidates having the greatest number of votes for President and Vice President shall be elected.

Section 5. The times, places, and manner of holding such elections and entitlement to inclusion on the ballot shall be determined by Congress.

Section 6. The Congress may by law provide for the case of the death or any other disqualification of any candidate for President or Vice President before the day on which the President-elect or Vice President-elect has been chosen; and for the case of a tie in any election.

Section 7: This article shall take effect one year after the first day of January following ratification.

This "second function" of any constitutional amendment could in some ways change the strategic calculus of the proponents. There may be some opponents who are leery of simply abolishing the Electoral College because they don't know what would replace it. But they might be won over if they see that the proposed replacement is fair and reasonable. This additional function of a constitutional amendment also alters the overall strategy for change in another way. If the other efforts to change the Electoral system through legislation, litigation, or a voting compact begin to hit their mark, then many in the political world may realize that the orderly process of amending the Constitution would have many advantages. And even if the proponents succeed in ending the Elector system through one of those other strategies, then Congress would probably still find a need to adopt a constitutional amendment to make sure that this change is permanent. In this sense, it may be more useful to think of a constitutional amendment as the last step of the process rather than the first.

✽ ✽ ✽

THE INTERSTATE COMPACT

The National Popular Vote Project (NPVP) is pushing another approach to changing the Electoral vote, but it is going at the problem from a different direction. The NPVP isn't trying to eliminate the Electoral College. Instead, it is attempting to use the mechanism of the Elector system to guarantee that the election will go to the winner of the popular vote. It's in some ways a startling idea, but its prospects for success seem rather good.

The NPVP is attempting to accomplish this feat through the use of an interstate compact that would guarantee that the winner of the national popular vote would end up being President. The idea behind the plan is to have each state that signs the NPVP Compact agree that it will cast its Electoral votes for the winner of the *national* popular vote, regardless of which candidate wins the popular vote in that particular state. Under the terms of the Compact, it will only go into operation when the NPVP has signed up enough states that together encompass at least a majority of the Electoral votes in the country. Thus, in order to put the Compact into operation, the proponents need to sign up states with a combined total of 270 Electoral votes.

As of last count, the Compact has been adopted by sixteen states representing 196 Electoral votes, which means it is now just 74 Electoral votes shy of the 270 needed for the Compact to go into effect. The most recent signatory state, Oregon, signed onto the Compact on June 12, 2019. There are several other states where it is now being considered, and in some of these states, the proposal has already passed at least one house of the state legislature. Of all the proposals to change the Electoral vote system, this one has the most momentum. (More information can be found at https://www.nationalpopularvote.com).

The NPVP plan is ingenious, and the sponsors have built a few safeguards into the design. The signatory states all agree that their chief election official shall "designate the presidential slate" of the candidate with the "largest national popular vote" as the Electors for that state. Thus, the Electors they put in place would be those who are already inclined to vote for that particular candidate. This would presumably minimize the prospect of revolt among the Electors. But the plan isn't foolproof. Although states can sign onto the Compact, they can also drop out of it. If a state leaves the Compact before July 20 in a presidential election year—and if that withdrawal would drop the total of all Electoral votes within the Compact below 270—then the Compact would not apply to that election. It's also not clear whether the Compact can go into effect without congressional approval. Article 1, Section 10, of the Constitution says that no state can enter into any "Agreement or Compact with another state" without the "consent of Congress." NPVP proponents, however, point to at least two Supreme Court cases suggesting congressional approval is not required unless the Compact acts to the "detriment of federal supremacy." They argue that federal supremacy is not at issue in this situation, so that requirement doesn't apply. What is clear, however, is that this is a unique use of the power of interstate compacts, and the result of any future litigation or challenge on these issues cannot be predicted with certainty.

How should citizen advocates for equal voting rights respond to the NPVP initiative? On the one hand, they should probably go all

out in support of the idea. If this Compact succeeds, then it guar-
antees that the candidate with the most votes nationwide becomes
President—an enormous victory for the fundamental right to an
equal vote. On the other hand, there are some people—or maybe
just me—who cringe at many of the assumptions behind the plan.
To get to the point where they can argue that states have the
power to enter into such a plan, the proponents have to assume an
outdated view of the role of Electors and an inflated view of state
control over those Electors—both of which run counter to more
than one hundred years of U.S. history. Perhaps the best way for
skeptics to reconcile themselves to this approach is to look at it as
a judo maneuver. The NPVP Compact is basically using the arcane
procedures of an out-of-date Elector system to flip the process on
its head and bring it into compliance with modern notions of equal
voting rights. That's good enough for me—at least for now.

   An unspoken assumption behind the NPVP proposal is this:
Once Americans have experienced a presidential election without
the dead hand of the Electoral College hanging over the outcome,
they will never want to go back. If so, then the Compact may just
be the first stop on the road to a more permanent solution. The
NPVP Compact, standing alone, might prove more unstable than
proponents of reform would like. Even if it goes into effect for one
or two elections, the public can never be quite sure that this new
system would continue to last into the future. Some states may
decide to drop out, throwing the Compact below the number of
Electoral votes needed. Or the number of Electoral votes needed
could shift or increase after the next Census, throwing the count
into disarray. Court challenges could throw the system off balance,
and recalcitrant Electors might occasionally decide to go their own
way. For that reason, the best result may be that the NPVP Compact will end up opening the door to a more permanent solution.

   If America is ready for change, then the NPVP might be just
the vehicle for pushing that reform forward and changing public
expectations. Once the "red state/blue state" and "safe state/swing
state" maps have disappeared from the screen, public attitudes
may shift. Voters living in Houston, Boston, Los Angeles, Atlanta,

and other places may suddenly realize that they are no longer marginalized, and they may get used to the idea. Once candidates begin to campaign throughout the entire country in search of votes, a new consensus may emerge. At that point, a constitutional amendment that permanently solves the problem may become a reality.

✿ ✿ ✿

CHALLENGES THROUGH THE COURTS

While many opponents of the Elector system support the Interstate Compact sponsored by the National Popular Vote Project or are pushing for a constitutional amendment—or, in many cases, doing both—lawsuits challenging the Elector system have been working their way through the legal system. These legal actions all approach the issue from different directions, and all of them are important. In each case, citizen advocates need to evaluate what is being sought and decide how it fits into an overall strategy for achieving equal voting rights.

1. Stopping the Winner-Take-All Rule

A group called Equal Votes (EV; https://equalvotes.us/) has filed suits in several federal courts claiming that the winner-take-all rules used by the states as part of the Electoral system are unconstitutional. Their claim is that this practice violates the right to an equal vote guaranteed under the 14th Amendment to the Constitution. The group contends that each state should award Electoral votes based on the percentage of the popular vote received by each candidate in that state. Equal Votes has filed four different lawsuits as test cases (in California, Massachusetts, Texas, and South Carolina). Two were dismissed, but the California case is now on appeal to the Ninth Circuit.

The proponents make the argument that the winner-take-all rules were not part of the original Electoral system but were instead added later by individual states without going through a constitutional approval process. They also point out that the winner-take-all rules grossly distort the popular vote and add greatly to the unfairness of the overall system. Both statements are clearly true. If equality and fairness are ever going to be achieved in the vote for President in the United Sates, then the winner-take-all rule has got to go.

If Equal Votes succeeds in any of these cases, it would be a big step forward. But it should be viewed as just one step in a larger process. Even with a victory, proponents of equal voting rights would sooner or later have to push for the elimination of the Electoral system altogether. The winner-take-all rule is a major flaw in the system, but it's not the only one. The unequal allocation of Electoral votes between the states is an equally big problem, and these cases don't address that part of the problem. Both issues will ultimately have to be dealt with to avoid a situation where the Electoral vote might continue to deviate from the popular vote.

The procedure that the Equal Votes team proposes is a step in the right direction, but that step alone might still leave several uncertainties. EV suggests that the percentage of the popular vote received by each candidate in a state should determine the number of Electors that the candidate receives in that state. But translating the percentage of the popular vote into a percentage of Electoral votes can create problems. For example, in 2016, Donald Trump received 38.1% of the popular vote in the state of Washington, and that percentage would theoretically yield 4.572 of Washington's 12 Electoral votes. Should the number of Electoral votes awarded to Trump have been 4 or 5 under that scenario? Right now, Electors only cast their votes in whole numbers. It might be theoretically possible to direct Electors to vote in percentage increments for different candidates, but that might require legislative action or further court rulings.

If a court or legislature were ever to eliminate the winner-take-all rule and require states to allocate Electors on the basis of a candidate's percentage of the vote in that state, then there would be a strong incentive for Congress to increase the size of the House of Representatives. Congress has the power to do so under Article I, Section 2, but it hasn't used that power in close to a century. Increasing the size of the House of Representatives is probably a good idea on its own merits because that would allow each member of Congress to have fewer constituents and, thus, be more responsive to their needs. But increasing the size of the House would automatically increase the number of Electors and might make an allocation of Electoral votes simpler in some instances.

A victory in these cases would be an important step forward. But even if the winner-take-all rule was eliminated, then there would still remain the possibility that a candidate with fewer popular votes might squeak out a victory in the Electoral College. More effort would still be needed to prevent that from happening. As with other victories that the proponents of change may achieve, a victory in these cases should be followed by an immediate effort to reform the system further. Reading between the lines, you get the idea that the EV supporters plan to do something like that if they win. A win would hopefully open the door to further action or a constitutional amendment.

2. Freedom for the Electors

Another group fighting the Elector system through the courts is Equal Citizens Foundation (https://www.equalcitizens.us). This group is challenging whether a state can control the votes of the Electors after they have been selected. Right now, the majority of states consider the Electors to be little more than robots who must vote the way that state law mandates. Some states even impose civil or criminal penalties if the Electors don't comply. But the

Equal Citizens Foundation takes the view that the Constitution allows Electors to vote however they want.

The foundation filed suit on behalf of an Elector who was chosen in 2016 by the Democratic Party in Colorado. After the November election, this Elector decided to switch his Electoral vote from Hillary Clinton to John Kasich at the time when the Electoral votes were due to be counted in December. But he ran up against a Colorado law that seemingly made it illegal for him to do so. The case went to the U.S. Court of Appeals for the Tenth Circuit. In *Baca v. Colorado*, No. 16-1482 (2016), the appellate court held that a state cannot control the way Electors cast their votes. Once Electors are appointed, the court said, they are independent agents who are not acting under state control:

> [S]tates appointing presidential electors are not selecting inferior state officials to assist in carrying out a function for which the state is ultimately responsible. Presidential electors exercise a federal function—not a state function—when casting their ballots. . . . From this we conclude that the states' power to appoint electors does not include the power to remove them or to nullify their votes.

Alexander Hamilton would probably have loved this decision. The only justification for Electors in his mind was their independence, and that's how he acted when he served in that role. The ruling in this case is not based on the 14th or 15th Amendments or on any of the Supreme Court cases having to do with modern voting rights. Instead, it derives from language going back to the founding of the republic. It simply reaffirms that the framers expected the Electors to act as independent agents in selecting a President.

If this case is sustained on appeal, then how would it affect the fight to achieve equal voting rights and ensure that the candidate with the most popular votes becomes President? Like many things in this struggle, this decision is probably best described as one step backward in order to take two steps forward. Giving Electors the right to vote their conscience in a modern-day setting does not solve the problem of unfairness that runs through our current method for electing a President. What it does, however, is undercut some of the assumptions behind the Elector system and help force a reassessment of how the President should be elected. If this case stands on appeal, it will serve to weaken the argument that the Elector system, as it is currently being administered, would ever have been considered constitutional—either in Hamilton's day or our own. In that sense, this case is one positive step on that path.

According to Larry Lessig, one of the driving forces behind this case, a Supreme Court decision affirming *Baca* might mean the following:

> If the Court decides as the 10th Circuit did, then that means that we as a nation need to decide whether we want to keep this system, or replace it—either through the National Popular Vote Compact, or through an Amendment to the Constitution. . . . [T]hen the race will be on to decide whether we keep the system the framers gave us, or decide as a nation—finally— to adopt something new.

We may get some idea of the impact of *Baca v. Colorado* in coming months because the Supreme Court announced on January 17, 2020, that it was granting a writ of certiorari in the case and thus taking it up for review. The most likely reason for the Court's action is that the Court of Appeals in another circuit had ruled on the same issue in recent months and reached the exact opposite conclusion. In *Chiafalo v. Washington*, the Court of Appeals upheld a penalty on an Elector who had attempted to change his vote before the Electoral votes were cast. It is this type of situation, where there is a conflict between two circuit courts, that the Supreme Court is most likely to take a case.

What would be the likely impact of a Supreme Court decision in this case? It's hard to guess, but one possibility is that it will have no impact at all. Colorado is arguing that that the decision should be reversed and that the case should then be dismissed as moot. They contend that Michael Baca, the plaintiff, has no standing to sue because the 2016 election is over, and he is under no immediate threat or penalty. If the Supreme Court buys that argument, then the case could be dismissed, and legally speaking, it will be as if it never happened. If the Supreme Court wants to duck the issue, then this is the best path for doing so.

But what if the Supreme Court decides to write a decision on the merits of the case? Because the Court took the case on appeal in January 2020, they might very well issue such a decision before the end of the term in June 2020. Such a ruling could be significant because any Supreme Court utterance would be scrutinized like a whole cupful of tea leaves to gauge the Supreme Court's long-term views about the Electoral College. But the real impact would likely only be felt in the long-term without having any real effect on the conduct of the 2020 presidential election. The issue before the Court is a narrow one: Can Electors vote their conscience, or can a state control how they are allowed to vote? It's an important question, but it's probably not going to change the outcome of any particular election. Electors are overwhelmingly party loyalists who are not likely to buck their party's choice for President, even if the Supreme Court says they have the right to do so.

What might be the longer-term implications of a decision in this case? No one can predict with any certainty what the Supreme Court is likely to say. But proponents of an equal vote for President need to be prepared to alter their strategy to follow whatever path seems more open to them after the decision is announced. If the Court upholds the *Baca* decision and says that a state can't control how Electors vote, then advocates for change might focus on other questionable practices by the states, such as delegating the choice of Electors to the political parties or allowing Electors to be chosen without conforming to any kind of standards. If, instead, the Court reverses the *Baca* decision and allows the states to control the way Electors vote, then proponents of change might see this as a green light for the NPVP strategy of a voting compact between states. If a state can control an Elector's vote, then arguably it is empowered to enter into a Compact with other states to ensure that all of their Electoral votes will be cast for the winner of the national popular vote. Either way, the fight will have to continue until equal voting rights are achieved for presidential elections.

3. The Direct Legal Challenge

It's probably just a matter of time before a legal team challenges the entire Elector system head-on. The lead in this kind of litigation could come from any one of several voting rights groups or similar organizations. Some of the most likely plaintiffs or plaintiffs' advocates would be the attorneys-general from large states whose citizens have been particularly hard hit by this system of unequal voting rights. It would be a bold litigation effort, and hopefully it could build on some of the arguments raised in this book. The main thrust might read something like this:

> *The election of President of the United States is a national election in all but name, and full voting rights should be protected for everyone voting in that election. The selection of the President was always intended to be a national process, and all historical and constitutional changes that have occurred since the founding of the country have made that even more clear and more urgent. The overwhelming majority of Americans view the presidential election process as the single most important political event in which they participate. Anything short of equal rights for every voter is a betrayal of the American public.*

This legal case could build on several of the points discussed earlier. The current Elector system is radically different from the system originally designed by the framers, and the changes that were made in that system by state legislatures never obtained constitutional approval. Moreover, modern-day Electors have been stripped of all useful purpose, and their only current function is to distort the results of the national popular vote for President. The argument would build on the fact that the current system locks into place a procedure that arbitrarily deprives voters in larger states of equal voting-power and systemically discriminates against minority voters throughout the country. The proponents in any such case would argue strongly that the current system is unconstitutional, under both the original language of the Constitution and the 14th, 15th, and subsequent amendments.

There's no doubt that such a broad-sweeping attack on the Elector system would face a difficult challenge in court, and that would be compounded by the conservative bent of the current Supreme Court. But that doesn't mean it shouldn't be pursued. Quite the contrary, a case like this could have a positive effect on all other strategies to change the system. The public awareness generated by such a case might help other efforts at change. If there is any political movement toward change in response to this type of litigation, then it will have served a useful purpose. This case would be the best vehicle for approaching the issues directly, forcing the defenders to testify and justify the Elector process, bringing the issues to the public, and discovering important background information. Such a lawsuit—or even the threat of it— might jolt many political leaders to take action that would allow them—rather than a panel of judges—to control the future of the system.

✿ ✿ ✿

ACTION BY CONGRESS

Congress has a key role to play in changing the Electoral system because it interacts in a crucial way with almost any proposal for change. Until now, there's been little discussion about the important role it can play in changing the Electoral system, but the reticence of Congress to act must change. Congress holds the big megaphone—it's the institution that can make an issue widely known throughout the country and draw attention to it. Beyond that, it can also lend a sense of seriousness and prestige to any other effort and provide it with essential support. Congress has the power and the resources to move in several directions at once in support of any effort to end the current system. It can provide the research and support that other efforts need, and it can act on its own through its legislative powers.

The following are some of the ways that Congress can interact with the efforts to change the Elector system.

Drafting the Constitutional Amendment

Constitutional amendments originate in Congress, and that gives Congress a crucial role in the terms of the debate. The usual discussion of a possible constitutional amendment looks at the issue from the tail end of the process (e.g., Will a particular state adopt the amendment that has just been dropped in its lap?). But the two houses of Congress have the power to shape the discussion. They can craft language of the amendment itself and, perhaps, find a way to make it palatable to the greatest number of states.

This power to shape the debate is particularly important when dealing with something as intricate as the Electoral system. A constitutional amendment would not only repeal the current system, but it would also have to replace it with a voting system that is more workable and acceptable. A key question would be this: How detailed should the amendment be? Should Congress propose a specific, self-operating election system that would replace the out-of-date language of the current system, or should it opt for a more general statement of principles that would leave the details of the election process to further congressional legislation? These are decisions that can make a difference in gathering support for the amendment.

Congressional Approval of the Interstate Compact

Congress can also play a key role in the effort to secure an Interstate Compact. The National Popular Vote Project is attempting to obtain commitments from states with enough Electoral votes to cast their votes for the winner for the national popular vote. What is still unresolved, however, is whether those states would have to obtain the approval of Congress for that Compact under Article I, Section 10, of the Constitution. Congress could solve that problem immediately. Whether congressional approval is required for the Compact or not, Congress could give a big boost to the process right now by adopting a resolution of support.

A resolution passed by both houses of Congress would probably remove any doubt as to the Compact's legality. But a vote by even one house at this point could be helpful. A persuasive resolution and report from the House of Representatives, for example, could give the NPVP Compact a huge publicity boost. It could also help sway state legislators who may be undecided about the wisdom of signing onto the Compact.

Congressional Investigation of the Elector System

The current system is in serious need of a congressional study. The disastrous effects of the Elector system have been ignored for years, and for the entire twentieth century, the guiding principle seems to have been "out of sight, out of mind." Because the Elector system hadn't altered the election results during that one-hundred-year period, no one bothered to look at it very closely. But those days are over. The impact of that system has been disastrous, and it's time for Congress to take a hard look at the harm it has caused. Not to be facetious, but the last group to look seriously at the Electoral system consisted of Alexander Hamilton, James Madison, and the other framers. But after 230 years, it's now clear that their ideas have been ignored. The system has fundamentally changed, and it is now crying out for another look.

Congress is in a unique position to do this. It has the resources, prestige, and public platform. It also has the subpoena power and access to government files that no other agency—public or private—can match. An investigation could be conducted by the two houses of Congress jointly, but it's also something that could be conducted by either house on its own. If the House of Representatives were to undertake to do this, the most likely vehicle would be a House select committee. This procedure has been used in the past for important investigations that cut across the jurisdiction of several standing committees. A thorough study could be used by Congress in future legislative efforts, but a more immediate use of such a report would be to help challengers put together a compelling case, either in court or in the political arena.

A study by a select committee could look at each presidential election over the last 230 years and determine how the Elector system affected the process. But it would also look at how the system of Electors has changed during that period and examine the step-by-step process that led to the erosion of the system. Important facts could be gleaned from a look at more recent issues, such as patterns of racial discrimination in presidential elections or foreign attacks on the election process. The committee should also look at the profound changes in the presidency since 1787 and evaluate how those changes affect the fairness of the election process and the perception of fairness that Americans have in their democratic institutions.

If such a congressional study is to be effective, then it would probably have to look at each election history in detail, focusing on granular issues that have often been overlooked in the past. Here are a few topics that a House select committee or other committee could start with:

- *Deviation from the original intent of the framers.* How did the current system evolve from the original system? What actions were taken by each state and in which years to change the Elector-selection process? What constitutional advice or procedures did they seek or follow in taking such actions?

- *Standards set by states for those serving as Electors.* What eligibility or disclosure standards have each of the state governments required of potential Electors? Do the states impose any standards at all on political parties before delegating to them the power to appoint and replace such Electors?

- *Identities of Electors.* What has been the history of Electors' names appearing on ballots? Which presidential elections listed the names of Electors listed on the ballot? In which elections were Electors first required to declare the name of the candidate they were supporting? In which elections did the names of Electors not appear at all on the ballot?

- *Percentage of voting-power discrimination.* What has been the percentage of voting-power discrimination (i.e., the difference in the number of voters it takes to elect one Elector) in each state vis-à-vis every other state in each general presidential election? What has been the percentage of this voting-power discrimination with respect to racial or ethnic minority voters?

- *Voting turnout.* What has been the correlation between the percentages of voter turnout in each state as compared with the winning margin in each state?

- *Campaigning in each state.* What has been the correlation between the numbers of campaign appearances by major candidates in each state during each general presidential election and the winning margin in each state?

- *Susceptibility to attack and manipulation.* What has been the correlation between the number of illegal efforts to manipulate voters or the voting process in each state during general presidential elections and the winning margin in each state?

Legislative Efforts by Congress to Change the System

Congress has the power under both the 14th and 15th Amendments to the Constitution to adopt legislation that could help put an end to voting discrimination in presidential elections. The 14th Amendment is the source of the "one person, one vote" rule that the Supreme Court has declared to be a fundamental right and that it has applied to every election. The 15th Amendment extends that equal right to vote even further by blocking anything that has a disparate impact on voters who are part of a racial minority. Both amendments also empower Congress to act. The 15th Amendment says in Article 2: "The Congress shall have the power to enforce this article by appropriate legislation." The 14th Amendment gives Congress that identical power in Section 5. It's time for Congress to consider using the powers that it has.

The question is just how far Congress can go in "enforcing" equal voting rights in presidential elections. The Supreme Court has tried to clarify this congressional power with respect to a different civil rights issue. The Court held that Congress "has been given the power 'to enforce,' not the power to determine what constitutes a constitutional violation" (*City of Boerne v. Flores*, 521 U.S. 507, 1997). In other words, Congress can enforce existing constitutional rights, but it can't create new ones. Because equal voting rights are in no sense new, the issue really is the extent of Congress's enforcement power within the context of the Electoral system. Could Congress reform those parts of the Electoral College that are not specifically described in the Constitution but are only regulated at this point by state legislation? Right now, for example, states have delegated the selection of Electors to political parties. This delegation process is something that each state has done on its own—it's not mentioned or even hinted at in the Constitution. If Congress determines that this state process has a negative effect on equal voting rights, could it use its enforcement power under Section 5 of the 14th Amendment to change or prevent such a practice?

The power that Congress can exercise in this context is also affected by judicial decisions and developments brought about by other efforts to reform the Electoral College system. In *Baca v. Colorado*, the case in which the Equal Citizen Foundation argued for the independence of Electors, the Court of Appeals said, "Presidential electors exercise a federal function—not a state function—when casting their ballots." If that case is upheld in the Supreme Court, then it suggests that Electors are subject to federal law in the exercise of their function. If that's true, then doesn't Congress have the power to ensure that Electors—like, for example, federal jurors—perform their job properly without any conflicts of interest, racial bias, or anything else that would be improper? And if *that's* true, then doesn't that suggest Congress has the power to regulate the way that states have delegated the appointment of Electors to political parties? As you push on the current relic of the original Elector system, you realize that one change can quickly lead to another.

Congress has yet to use the powers granted to them under the 14th and 15th Amendments, but they are powers that could be decisive. Congress already has the power to affect the Elector system by investigation, and it also has the power to propose changes in the system through a constitutional amendment. But it may be that its most significant power is the power to change the system through legislation.

☼ ☼ ☼

PEOPLE POWER

None of these changes are likely to happen unless American citizens demand that they happen. The Electoral system has hidden itself far too long in the recesses of our politics, and it has managed to remain there because the public has not demanded that it be brought out into the light of day.

This must change. Community groups can take up the issue. In my own hometown of Mill Valley, California, a local group called Mill Valley Seniors for Peace decided on their own to start working on the Elector issue. We need hundreds of organizations like this around the country making the same effort. Many larger progressive groups are starting to talk about eliminating the Elector system, but they must move this issue to the top of their agenda and devote sufficient resources to the effort. Politicians are now starting to discuss ways to end the Elector system, but they need to get far beyond the discussion stage. They either need to take strong action or expect to find the members of local progressive groups camping out in their waiting rooms. What to do immediately?

- Contact your local state senator and assembly representatives and urge them to support both a constitutional amendment and your state's adherence to the NPVP Compact.
- Contact your U.S. senator and congressperson and ask them to set up a select committee to investigate thoroughly the Elector system and to follow up on the results of that investigation.
- Contact your state attorney-general and urge him or her to file an action on behalf of the citizens of your state to enforce your equal voting rights.

Proponents of change need to be persistent. There are a few groups already organized around the idea of ending the Elector system, and probably all those organizations are worthy of your support, but the effort can't stop there. Other larger, mainstream organizations need to be brought into the fight. If any such organization sends you a solicitation for funds, you should check into what that organization is doing on this issue. If there is no such action plan, then perhaps the solicitation letter should be sent back with a polite suggestion that they do better next time.

Proponents of change must be smart and flexible. The different strategies for change overlap each other in many ways, and proponents need to keep an eye on how each such effort fits into the overall push for change. The goal is to secure equal voting rights for everyone in presidential elections and to make sure that the candidate with the most votes wins. It's important to evaluate each of the many tactics to make sure it is advancing those goals.

Proponents of changing the Electoral system have the moral high ground, and they should never give it up. They are working for nothing less than finally bringing a true democracy to America, and there's no better cause than that.

AFTERWORD

The Electoral College in the Time of Pandemic

On April 7, 2020, voters in Wisconsin stood in line for up to three hours, endured a rainstorm, risked their health in the middle of a pandemic, and waited for a turn at one of only 2% of the former polling stations that were still open. It was a show of bravery by the voters that was matched only by the callousness of the politicians who forced them into that situation.

The election could have been delayed. Or the time for voting could easily have been extended, as both the governor and a federal district tried to do. But the U.S. Supreme Court prevented that from happening, provoking this scathing dissent from Justice Ruth Bader Ginsburg:

> Either they will have to brave the polls, endangering their own and other's safety, or they will lose their right to vote, through no fault of their own. That is a matter of utmost importance— to the constitutional rights of Wisconsin's citizens, the integrity of the State's election process, and in this extraordinary time, the health of the Nation.

Why did this happen? The presidential primary election was basically over at that point, and the only serious contest was for a single seat on the Wisconsin Supreme Court. Why did this seemingly local issue provoke two legislative sessions, a governor's emergency order, a presidential pronouncement, and four court decisions? There were plenty of heartless politicians to blame for this debacle, but there was also one institutional culprit: the Electoral College.

In 2016, Donald Trump won the popular vote in Wisconsin by only 22,748 votes. However, that narrow margin in Wisconsin was linked to a sharp and sudden decrease in voter turnout. While the neighboring states all showed an increase in voting over the prior presidential election, Wisconsin showed a drop of 92,284 votes from 2012 to 2016. Political experts worried that such a decrease in voting would probably occur when Wisconsin embarked on the aggressive enforcement of a new law on voter IDs. That effort turned away as many as 200,000 voters—mostly African Americans—and was probably decisive in determining the outcome of the Wisconsin vote. Since that draconian law had received the blessing of the Wisconsin Supreme Court going into the 2016 election, is it any wonder that the group seeking the same result in the next presidential election would move heaven and earth to depress the vote in this April election to help keep its majority on the state Supreme Court?

But the Electoral College has a way of turning any such statewide issue into a matter of crucial national importance. Trump's margin of 22,748 votes in Wisconsin in 2016 represented only about 0.3% of Clinton's nationwide popular-vote margin of 2,868,692—a small dent in her otherwise successful vote-getting effort throughout the nation. But as small as it was, Trump's margin in Wisconsin gave him that state's ten Electoral votes, which represented about 24% of his winning margin in the national Electoral vote. In other words, a small difference in the popular-vote margin in Wisconsin was magnified way out of proportion in the Electoral vote count. In fact, the Wisconsin margin had an impact that was about *eighty times* higher in the national *Electoral* vote than in the national *popular* vote.

If you are a political insider, the health risk to voters must seem like a small price to pay in order to maintain that sort of advantage in the Electoral College.

ABOUT THE AUTHOR

Bill Petrocelli is a lawyer, author, and co-owner with his wife, Elaine, of the nationally known bookstore Book Passage in Corte Madera and San Francisco, California.

He is the author of four books. *Low Profile: How to Avoid the Privacy Invaders*, published in 1980, was one of the first books to discuss abuses of data collection by government and businesses and the future implications of computerized record-keeping. *Sexual Harassment on the Job: What It Is and How to Stop It* was co-authored by Barbara Kate Repa and published in 1992. It was the first book published on the subject of stopping workplace harassment and sexual violence. *The Circle of Thirteen*, a novel published in 2013, had as its theme the coming empowerment of women. Novelist Lisa See called it "a true celebration of women in the face of great odds." *Through the Bookstore Window* was published in 2018. *Foreword Magazine* calls this novel "an unusual, rewarding take on the nature of memory: how it haunts and heals, how single moments set the future in motion, and how it binds survivors together in ways they seldom expect."